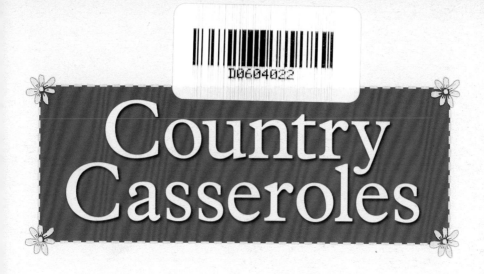

Country Casseroles

Publications International, Ltd.

Pictured on the front cover: Family-Style Frankfurters with Rice and Red Beans *(page 32).*
Pictured on the back cover *(top to bottom):* Cheddar Apple Breakfast Lasagna *(page 10)* and Chili Wagon Wheel Casserole *(page 40).*

ISBN-13: 978-1-60553-706-1
ISBN-10: 1-60553-706-3

Library of Congress Control Number: 2010923077

Manufactured in China.

8 7 6 5 4 3 2 1

Microwave Cooking: Microwave ovens vary in wattage. Use the cooking times as guidelines and check for doneness before adding more time.

Preparation/Cooking Times: Preparation times are based on the approximate amount of time required to assemble the recipe before cooking, baking, chilling or serving. These times include preparation steps such as measuring, chopping and mixing. The fact that some preparations and cooking can be done simultaneously is taken into account. Preparation of optional ingredients and serving suggestions is not included.

Publications International, Ltd.

Table of Contents

Brunch Bakes 4

Family Favorites 26

Harvest Helpings 50

Farmhand Feasts 72

Simple Suppers 94

Potluck Perfection 116

Acknowledgments 139

Index 140

Brunch Bakes

Crustless Salmon & Broccoli Quiche

Makes 4 servings

    3 eggs
 ¼ cup chopped green onions
 ¼ cup plain yogurt
    2 teaspoons all-purpose flour
    1 teaspoon dried basil
 ⅛ teaspoon salt
 ⅛ teaspoon black pepper
 ¾ cup frozen broccoli florets, thawed and drained
 ⅓ cup (3 ounces) drained and flaked canned salmon
    2 tablespoons grated Parmesan cheese
    1 plum tomato, thinly sliced
 ¼ cup fresh bread crumbs

1. Preheat oven to 375°F. Lightly coat 1½-quart casserole or 9-inch deep-dish pie plate with nonstick cooking spray.

2. Whisk eggs, green onions, yogurt, flour, basil, salt and pepper in medium bowl until well blended. Stir in broccoli, salmon and cheese. Spread evenly in prepared casserole. Top with tomato slices and sprinkle with bread crumbs.

3. Bake 20 to 25 minutes or until knife inserted into center comes out clean. Let stand 5 minutes before serving.

Apple-Cranberry Kugel

Makes 6 servings

8 ounces uncooked extra-wide egg noodles
6 egg yolks
¾ cup sugar
1⅓ cups milk
1⅓ cups whipping cream
1 teaspoon vanilla
¼ teaspoon ground cinnamon
2 cups sliced apples
1 cup dried cranberries

1. Preheat oven to 350°F. Lightly coat 8-inch square baking dish with nonstick cooking spray.

2. Cook noodles according to package directions; drain. Rinse under cold water; drain well.

3. Whisk egg yolks and sugar in large bowl until thick and pale yellow. Whisk in milk, cream, vanilla and cinnamon.

4. Toss noodles, apples and cranberries in separate large bowl until combined. Transfer to prepared baking dish. Pour 3 cups egg mixture over noodles. Cover with foil. Bake 55 minutes or just until set. (The middle will set as it cools.)

5. Cook and stir remaining egg mixture in small saucepan over low heat 8 minutes or until mixture coats back of spoon. Drizzle over kugel.

Apple-Cranberry Kugel

Roasted Pepper and Sourdough Brunch Casserole

Makes 6 to 8 servings

3 cups sourdough bread cubes
1 jar (12 ounces) roasted red pepper strips, drained
1 cup (4 ounces) shredded sharp Cheddar cheese
1 cup (4 ounces) shredded Monterey Jack cheese
1 cup cottage cheese
6 eggs
1 cup milk
¼ cup chopped fresh cilantro
¼ teaspoon black pepper

1. Lightly coat 11×7-inch baking dish with nonstick cooking spray. Place bread cubes in prepared baking dish. Arrange roasted peppers evenly over bread cubes; sprinkle with Cheddar and Monterey Jack cheeses.

2. Place cottage cheese in food processor or blender; process until smooth. Add eggs and milk; process just until blended. Pour over ingredients in baking dish. Sprinkle with cilantro and black pepper. Cover; refrigerate 4 to 12 hours.

3. Preheat oven to 375°F. Bake 40 minutes or until center is set and top is golden brown.

Roasted Pepper and Sourdough Brunch Casserole

Cheddar Apple Breakfast Lasagna

Makes 6 servings

1 cup sour cream
⅓ cup brown sugar
2 packages (9 ounces each) frozen French toast
½ pound sliced ham
2 cups (8 ounces) SARGENTO® ARTISAN BLENDS™ Shredded
  Double Cheddar Cheese, divided
1 can (20 ounces) apple pie filling
1 cup granola with raisins

BLEND sour cream and brown sugar in small bowl; chill until serving time.

PLACE 6 French toast slices in greased 13×9-inch baking pan. Layer ham, 1½ cups cheese and remaining 6 slices of French toast in pan. Spread with apple filling; sprinkle with granola.

BAKE in preheated 350°F oven 25 minutes. Top with remaining cheese; bake 5 minutes more or until cheese is melted and casserole is hot. Serve with sour cream mixture.

Prep Time: 20 minutes • Cook Time: 30 minutes

Cheddar Apple Breakfast Lasagna

Spinach Sensation

Makes 4 to 6 servings

½ pound bacon slices
1 cup sour cream
3 eggs, separated
2 tablespoons all-purpose flour
⅛ teaspoon black pepper
1 package (10 ounces) frozen chopped spinach, thawed and squeezed dry
½ cup (2 ounces) shredded sharp Cheddar cheese
½ cup plain dry bread crumbs
1 tablespoon butter, melted

1. Preheat oven to 350°F. Lightly coat 2-quart round baking dish with nonstick cooking spray.

2. Place bacon in single layer in large skillet; cook over medium heat until crisp. Remove from skillet; drain on paper towels. Crumble and set aside.

3. Whisk sour cream, egg yolks, flour and pepper in large bowl until blended. Beat egg whites in medium bowl with electric mixer at high speed until stiff peaks form. Stir one fourth of egg whites into sour cream mixture; fold in remaining egg whites.

4. Arrange half of spinach in prepared baking dish. Top with half of sour cream mixture. Sprinkle with ¼ cup cheese. Top evenly with bacon. Repeat layers, ending with remaining ¼ cup cheese.

5. Combine bread crumbs and butter in small bowl; sprinkle evenly over top. Bake 30 to 35 minutes or until center is set. Let stand 5 minutes before serving.

Spinach Sensation

Blueberry-Orange French Toast Casserole

Makes 4 to 6 servings

6 slices whole wheat bread, cut into 1-inch pieces
1 cup fresh (not frozen) blueberries
½ cup milk
¼ cup sugar
2 eggs
4 egg whites
1 tablespoon grated orange peel
½ teaspoon vanilla

1. Preheat oven to 350°F. Coat 8-inch square baking dish with nonstick cooking spray. Combine bread and blueberries in prepared baking dish.

2. Whisk milk and sugar in medium bowl until sugar is dissolved. Whisk in eggs, egg whites, orange peel and vanilla. Pour over bread mixture; toss to coat. Let stand 5 minutes.

3. Bake 40 to 45 minutes or until top of bread is browned and center is almost set. Let stand 5 minutes before serving.

TIP: Whole wheat bread gives this delicious casserole a richer flavor, as well as more fiber and other nutrients. However, in a pinch, any kind of bread can be used.

Blueberry-Orange French Toast Casserole

Breakfast Bake

Makes 8 servings

1 pound ground pork sausage
1 teaspoon Italian seasoning
½ teaspoon salt
6 eggs
2 cups milk
½ cup **CREAM OF WHEAT®** Hot Cereal (Instant, 1-minute, 2½-minute or 10-minute cook time), uncooked
1 teaspoon **TRAPPEY'S®** Red Devil™ Cayenne Pepper Sauce
4 cups cubed bread (potato bread recommended)
2 cups Cheddar cheese, shredded

1. Brown sausage in skillet, pressing with fork or spatula to crumble as it cooks. Sprinkle on Italian seasoning and salt; set aside.

2. Combine eggs, milk, Cream of Wheat and pepper sauce in large mixing bowl; mix well. Add cooked sausage and bread; toss to combine. Pour mixture into 13×9-inch casserole pan; cover. Refrigerate at least 4 hours or overnight.

3. Preheat oven to 350°F. Remove cover and sprinkle cheese over casserole. Cover pan with aluminum foil; bake 30 minutes. Remove foil; bake 15 minutes longer. Serve warm.

Prep Time: 30 minutes

Breakfast Bake

Egg and Green Chile Rice Casserole

Makes 4 servings

¾ cup uncooked instant brown rice
½ cup chopped green onions
½ teaspoon ground cumin
1 can (4 ounces) chopped mild green chiles, drained
⅛ teaspoon salt
4 eggs, beaten
½ cup (2 ounces) shredded sharp Cheddar cheese or Mexican
  cheese blend
¼ cup pico de gallo
1 lime, cut into wedges

1. Preheat oven to 350°F. Lightly coat 8-inch square baking dish with nonstick cooking spray.

2. Cook rice according to package directions. Remove from heat; stir in green onions and cumin. Transfer to prepared baking dish.

3. Sprinkle chiles and salt evenly over rice mixture. Pour eggs evenly over top. Bake 30 to 35 minutes or until center is set.

4. Sprinkle with cheese. Bake 3 minutes or until cheese is melted. Let stand 5 minutes. Serve with pico de gallo and lime wedges.

TIP: Fully or partially cooked and then dehydrated,
instant brown rice takes just minutes to prepare.
It's a great way to incorporate the nutritional benefits
associated with brown rice into your diet
when time is limited.

Egg and Green Chile Rice Casserole

Bacon and Eggs Brunch Casserole

Makes 6 servings

1 tube (8 ounces) refrigerated crescent roll dough
6 eggs
½ cup milk
1 cup (4 ounces) SARGENTO® Chef Style Shredded Mild Cheddar
    Cheese
8 slices bacon, diced and cooked crisp

SPRAY a 13×9-inch baking pan with non-stick cooking spray. Unroll dough and press into bottom of pan. Bake in preheated 350°F oven 10 minutes.

BEAT together eggs and milk in medium bowl. Pour over partially-baked dough. Sprinkle with cheese and bacon; return to oven and bake 25 minutes more or until center is set.

Ham & Cheese Grits Soufflé

Makes 4 to 6 servings

3 cups water
¾ cup quick-cooking grits
½ teaspoon salt
½ cup (2 ounces) shredded mozzarella cheese
2 ounces ham, finely chopped
2 tablespoons minced fresh chives
2 eggs, separated
    Dash hot pepper sauce

1. Preheat oven to 375°F. Grease 1½-quart soufflé dish.

2. Bring water to a boil in medium saucepan; stir in grits and salt. Cook and stir 5 minutes or until thickened. Stir in cheese, ham, chives, egg yolks and hot pepper sauce.

3. Beat egg whites in small bowl until stiff but not dry; fold into grits mixture. Spoon into prepared soufflé dish. Bake 30 minutes or until puffed and golden. Serve immediately.

Bacon and Eggs Brunch Casserole

Fruited Corn Pudding

Makes 8 servings

> 5 cups thawed frozen corn, divided
> 5 eggs
> ½ cup milk
> 1½ cups whipping cream
> ⅓ cup unsalted butter, melted and cooled
> 1 teaspoon vanilla
> ½ teaspoon salt
> ¼ teaspoon ground nutmeg
> 3 tablespoons finely chopped dried apricots
> 3 tablespoons dried cranberries or raisins
> 3 tablespoons finely chopped dates
> 2 tablespoons finely chopped dried pears or other dried fruit

1. Preheat oven to 350°F. Grease 13×9-inch baking dish.

2. Combine 3½ cups corn, eggs and milk in food processor; process until almost smooth.

3. Transfer corn mixture to large bowl. Add cream, butter, vanilla, salt and nutmeg; stir until well blended.

4. Add remaining 1½ cups corn, apricots, cranberries, dates and pears; stir well. Pour mixture into prepared baking dish.

5. Bake 50 to 60 minutes or until center is set and top begins to brown. Let stand 10 to 15 minutes before serving.

Fruited Corn Pudding

Egg & Sausage Casserole

Makes 6 servings

½ pound pork sausage
3 tablespoons butter, divided
2 tablespoons all-purpose flour
¼ teaspoon salt
¼ teaspoon black pepper
1¼ cups milk
2 cups frozen hash brown potatoes
4 eggs, hard-cooked and sliced
½ cup cornflake crumbs
¼ cup sliced green onions

1. Preheat oven to 350°F. Lightly coat 2-quart oval baking dish with nonstick cooking spray.

2. Brown sausage in large skillet over medium-high heat 6 to 8 minutes, stirring to break up meat. Drain on paper towels.

3. Melt 2 tablespoons butter in same skillet over medium heat. Stir in flour, salt and pepper until smooth. Gradually stir in milk; cook and stir until thickened. Add sausage, potatoes and eggs; stir until blended. Transfer to prepared baking dish.

4. Melt remaining 1 tablespoon butter in small saucepan over low heat. Add cornflake crumbs; stir until combined. Sprinkle evenly over casserole.

5. Bake 30 minutes or until hot and bubbly. Sprinkle with green onions just before serving.

Egg & Sausage Casserole

Family Favorites

Chicken Pot Pie with Onion Biscuits

Makes 6 servings

1 package (1.8 ounces) classic white sauce mix
2¾ cups milk, divided
¼ teaspoon dried thyme leaves
1 package (10 ounces) frozen peas and carrots, thawed
1 package (10 ounces) roasted carved chicken breast, cut into bite-size pieces
1 cup all-purpose baking mix
1⅓ cups *French's®* French Fried Onions, divided
½ cup (2 ounces) shredded Cheddar cheese

1. Preheat oven to 400°F. Prepare white sauce mix according to package directions with 2¼ cups milk; stir in thyme. Mix vegetables, chicken and prepared white sauce in shallow 2-quart casserole.

2. Combine baking mix, ⅔ *cup* French Fried Onions and remaining ½ cup milk in medium bowl until blended. Drop 6 to 8 spoonfuls of dough over chicken mixture.

3. Bake 25 minutes or until biscuits are golden. Sprinkle biscuits with cheese and remaining ⅔ *cup* onions. Bake 3 minutes or until cheese is melted and onions are golden.

Variation: For added Cheddar flavor, substitute *French's®* Cheddar French Fried Onions for the original flavor.

Prep Time: 15 minutes • **Cook Time:** 33 minutes

Pork and Corn Bread Stuffing Casserole

Makes 4 servings

½ teaspoon paprika
¼ teaspoon salt
¼ teaspoon garlic powder
¼ teaspoon black pepper
4 bone-in pork chops
2 tablespoons butter
1½ cups chopped onions
¾ cup thinly sliced celery
¾ cup matchstick carrots*
¼ cup chopped fresh Italian parsley
1 can (about 14 ounces) chicken broth
4 cups corn bread stuffing mix

*Matchstick carrots (sometimes called shredded carrots) can be found near other prepared vegetables in the supermarket produce section.

1. Preheat oven to 350°F. Lightly coat 13×9-inch baking dish with nonstick cooking spray.

2. Combine paprika, salt, garlic powder and pepper in small bowl. Season both sides of pork chops with paprika mixture.

3. Melt butter in large skillet over medium-high heat. Add pork chops; cook 4 minutes or just until browned, turning once. Transfer to plate; set aside.

4. Add onions, celery, carrots and parsley to same skillet; cook and stir 4 minutes or until onions are translucent. Add broth; bring to a boil. Remove from heat; add stuffing mix and fluff with fork.

5. Transfer stuffing mixture to prepared baking dish. Top with pork chops. Cover; bake 25 minutes or until pork is barely pink in center.

Variation: For a one-dish meal, use an ovenproof skillet. Place browned pork chops on mixture in skillet; cover and bake as directed.

Pork and Corn Bread Stuffing Casserole

Pizza Roll-Ups

Makes 8 servings

½ pound lean ground beef or turkey
1 small onion, chopped
¾ teaspoon garlic salt
¼ teaspoon crushed red pepper flakes
1 jar (28 ounces) pasta sauce with mushrooms, divided
2 cups (8 ounces) SARGENTO® Fancy Shredded 6 Cheese Italian
   Cheese, divided
8 long (6 ounces) lasagna noodles, cooked and drained

BROWN ground beef and onion in large skillet. Pour off drippings. Sprinkle meat mixture with garlic salt and pepper flakes. Remove from heat; stir in ½ cup pasta sauce and 1½ cups cheese.

SPOON 1 cup pasta sauce into 2-quart rectangular baking dish. Spoon ¼ cup meat mixture down center of each lasagna noodle; roll up and place, seam-side down, in baking dish. Spoon remaining sauce over roll-ups.

COVER with foil; bake in preheated 375°F oven 35 minutes or until heated through. Remove from oven; uncover and sprinkle with remaining cheese. Let stand 5 minutes before serving.

Prep Time: 20 minutes • **Cook Time:** 35 minutes

Pizza Roll-Ups

Family-Style Frankfurters with Rice and Red Beans

Makes 6 servings

1 tablespoon vegetable oil
1 onion, chopped
½ green bell pepper, chopped
2 cloves garlic, minced
1 can (about 15 ounces) red kidney beans, rinsed and drained
1 can (about 15 ounces) Great Northern beans, rinsed and drained
½ pound beef frankfurters, cut into ¼-inch-thick pieces
1 cup uncooked instant brown rice
1 cup vegetable broth
¼ cup packed brown sugar
¼ cup ketchup
3 tablespoons dark molasses
1 tablespoon Dijon mustard

1. Preheat oven to 350°F. Lightly coat 13×9-inch baking dish with nonstick cooking spray.

2. Heat oil in Dutch oven over medium-high heat. Add onion, bell pepper and garlic; cook and stir 2 minutes or until tender.

3. Add beans, frankfurters, rice, broth, brown sugar, ketchup, molasses and mustard; stir to blend. Transfer to prepared baking dish.

4. Cover tightly with foil; bake 30 minutes or until rice is tender.

Family-Style Frankfurters with Rice and Red Beans

Velveeta® Tuna Noodle Casserole

Makes 8 servings

WHAT YOU NEED

4 cups egg noodles, cooked, drained
1 package (16 ounces) frozen peas and carrots
2 cans (6 ounces each) tuna, drained, flaked
1 can (10¾ ounces) condensed cream of mushroom soup
⅓ cup milk
¾ pound (12 ounces) **VELVEETA®** Pasteurized Prepared Cheese
Product, cut into ½-inch cubes
1 can (2.8 ounces) French fried onion rings

MAKE IT

1. HEAT oven to 400°F. Combine all ingredients except onions in 13×9-inch baking dish; cover with foil.

2. BAKE 45 minutes or until heated through; stir.

3. TOP with onions.

Variation: For a lighter dish, prepare using reduced-fat condensed cream of mushroom soup and VELVEETA® 2% Milk Pasteurized Prepared Cheese Product.

Prep Time: 20 minutes • **Total Time:** 55 minutes

Velveeta® Tuna Noodle Casserole

City Pork BBQ Casserole

Makes 6 to 8 servings

2 tablespoons vegetable oil
6 to 8 boneless pork chops (about 2 pounds), cut into bite-size pieces
¼ cup chopped onion
2 cloves garlic, minced
2 cups water
2 cups uncooked instant white rice
1 bottle (12 ounces) chili sauce
1 cup ketchup
½ cup packed brown sugar
2 tablespoons honey
1 tablespoon Worcestershire sauce
1 tablespoon hot pepper jelly
1 teaspoon ground ginger
1 teaspoon liquid smoke (optional)
½ teaspoon curry powder
¼ teaspoon black pepper
2 cups (8 ounces) shredded mozzarella cheese

1. Preheat oven to 350°F.

2. Heat oil in large skillet over medium-high heat. Add pork; cook and stir 10 to 15 minutes or until browned and barely pink in center. Add onion and garlic; cook and stir until tender. Drain fat.

3. Meanwhile, bring water to a boil in small saucepan. Stir in rice; cover. Remove from heat; let stand 5 minutes or until water is absorbed.

4. Combine chili sauce, ketchup, brown sugar, honey, Worcestershire sauce, hot pepper jelly, ginger, liquid smoke, if desired, curry powder and black pepper in medium saucepan; bring to a boil over medium-high heat. Reduce heat to low; cover and simmer 10 minutes, stirring occasionally.

5. Combine pork mixture, rice and chili sauce mixture in 2½-quart casserole; mix well. Bake 15 to 20 minutes. Top with cheese; bake 5 minutes or until cheese is melted. Let stand 5 minutes before serving.

City Pork BBQ Casserole

Homestyle Chicken & Rice Casserole

Makes 4 servings

1 cup long grain white rice
1 can (14 ounces) chicken broth
¾ cup chopped onion
2 cups small broccoli florets
4 (2½ pounds) bone-in chicken breast halves
1 teaspoon paprika
1 teaspoon thyme leaves
1 teaspoon garlic salt
2 cups (8 ounces) SARGENTO® Fancy Shredded Mild Cheddar Cheese

COMBINE rice, broth, onion and broccoli in 11×7-inch baking pan. Place chicken over rice mixture. Combine paprika, thyme and garlic salt in small bowl; sprinkle over chicken.

COVER with foil; bake in preheated 375°F oven 40 minutes. Uncover; bake 15 minutes more or until liquid is absorbed, rice is tender and chicken is cooked through.

SPRINKLE chicken and rice with cheese. Bake 5 minutes more or until cheese is melted.

Prep Time: 15 minutes • **Cook Time:** 60 minutes

Homestyle Chicken & Rice Casserole

Chili Wagon Wheel Casserole

Makes 4 to 6 servings

  8 ounces uncooked wagon wheel or other pasta
    Nonstick cooking spray
  1 pound ground turkey
  ¾ cup chopped onion
  ¾ cup chopped green bell pepper
  1 can (about 14 ounces) stewed tomatoes
  1 can (8 ounces) tomato sauce
  ½ teaspoon black pepper
  ¼ teaspoon ground allspice
  ½ cup (2 ounces) shredded Cheddar cheese

1. Preheat oven to 350°F. Cook pasta according to package directions until almost tender; drain well.

2. Lightly coat large nonstick skillet with cooking spray; heat over medium-high heat. Add turkey; cook and stir 5 minutes or until no longer pink. Add onion and bell pepper; cook and stir until tender.

3. Stir in tomatoes, tomato sauce, black pepper and allspice; cook 2 minutes. Stir in pasta. Spoon mixture into 2½-quart casserole. Sprinkle with cheese.

4. Bake 20 to 25 minutes or until heated through.

TIP: Allspice has a complex flavor resembling a blend of cinnamon, nutmeg and cloves. It can be used to add depth to savory dishes or baked goods.

Chili Wagon Wheel Casserole

Hearty Sausage & Rice Casserole

Makes 6 servings

1 pound bulk pork sausage
1 package (8 ounces) sliced mushrooms
2 stalks celery, coarsely chopped (about 1 cup)
1 large red pepper, coarsely chopped (about 1 cup)
1 large onion, coarsely chopped (about 1 cup)
1 teaspoon dried thyme leaves, crushed
½ teaspoon dried marjoram leaves, crushed
1 box (6 ounces) seasoned long grain and wild rice mix
1¾ cups SWANSON® Chicken Stock
1 can (10¾ ounces) CAMPBELL'S® Condensed Cream of Mushroom
    Soup (Regular or 98% Fat Free)
1 cup shredded Cheddar cheese (about 4 ounces)

1. Cook the sausage in a 12-inch skillet over medium-high heat until it's well browned, stirring often to separate meat. Pour off any fat.

2. Add the mushrooms, celery, pepper, onion, thyme, marjoram and seasoning packet from the rice mix to the skillet and cook until the vegetables are tender-crisp.

3. Stir the sausage mixture, stock, soup, rice mix and ½ **cup** cheese in a 3-quart shallow baking dish. Cover the baking dish.

4. Bake at 375°F. for 1 hour or until the sausage is cooked through and the rice is tender. Stir the sausage mixture before serving. Sprinkle with the remaining cheese.

Kitchen Tip: For an extra-special touch, substitute 1 package (8 ounces) baby portobello mushrooms, sliced, for the sliced mushrooms.

Prep Time: 30 minutes • **Bake Time:** 1 hour

Hearty Sausage & Rice Casserole

Stroganoff Casserole

Makes 8 servings

1 package (16 ounces) egg noodles
2 cans (10¾ ounces each) condensed cream of mushroom soup, undiluted
1 container (8 ounces) sour cream
½ cup milk
1 pound ground beef
2 cans (6 ounces each) sliced mushrooms, undrained
1 package (8 ounces) cream cheese
1 package (about 1 ounce) gravy mix

1. Preheat oven to 350°F.

2. Cook noodles according to package directions in 4-quart Dutch oven. Drain well; return to Dutch oven.

3. Add soups, sour cream and milk; stir to combine. Cover and keep warm.

4. Brown beef in large skillet over medium-high heat 6 to 8 minutes, stirring to break up meat. Drain fat.

5. Add mushrooms, cream cheese and gravy mix to beef; stir until blended. Transfer beef mixture to Dutch oven; stir until noodles are coated.

6. Bake 30 minutes or until heated through.

Stroganoff Casserole

Louisiana Seafood Bake

Makes 4 servings

1 can (14½ ounces) whole tomatoes, undrained and cut up
1 can (8 ounces) tomato sauce
1 cup water
1 cup sliced celery
⅔ cup uncooked regular rice
1⅓ cups *French's®* French Fried Onions, divided
1 teaspoon *Frank's® RedHot®* Original Cayenne Pepper Sauce
½ teaspoon garlic powder
¼ teaspoon dried oregano, crumbled
¼ teaspoon dried thyme, crumbled
½ pound white fish, thawed if frozen and cut into 1-inch chunks
1 can (4 ounces) shrimp, drained
⅓ cup sliced pitted ripe olives
¼ cup (1 ounce) grated Parmesan cheese

Preheat oven to 375°F. In 1½-quart casserole, combine tomatoes, tomato sauce, water, celery, uncooked rice, ⅔ *cup* French Fried Onions and seasonings. Bake, covered, at 375°F for 20 minutes. Stir in fish, shrimp and olives. Bake, covered, 20 minutes or until heated through. Top with cheese and remaining ⅔ *cup* onions; bake, uncovered, 3 minutes or until onions are golden brown.

Microwave Directions: In 2-quart microwave-safe casserole, prepare rice mixture as above. Cook, covered, on HIGH 15 minutes, stirring rice halfway through cooking time. Add fish, shrimp and olives. Cook, covered, 12 to 14 minutes or until rice is cooked. Stir casserole halfway through cooking time. Top with cheese and remaining ⅔ *cup* onions; cook, uncovered, 1 minute. Let stand 5 minutes.

Louisiana Seafood Bake

Rainbow Casserole

Makes 4 to 6 servings

 5 potatoes, peeled and cut into thin slices
 1 pound ground beef
 1 onion, halved and thinly sliced
   Salt and black pepper
 1 can (about 28 ounces) stewed tomatoes, drained, juice reserved
 1 cup frozen peas *or* 1 can (about 6 ounces) peas, drained

1. Preheat oven to 350°F. Lightly coat 3-quart casserole with nonstick cooking spray.

2. Combine potatoes and enough salted water to cover in large saucepan. Bring to a boil over high heat. Reduce heat to low; simmer 15 minutes or until almost tender. Drain. Meanwhile, brown beef in large skillet over medium-high heat 6 to 8 minutes, stirring to break up meat. Drain fat.

3. Layer half of beef, half of potatoes, half of onion, salt, pepper, half of tomatoes and half of peas in prepared casserole. Repeat layers. Add reserved tomato juice.

4. Cover; bake 40 minutes or until most of liquid is absorbed.

Chili Dog Casserole

Makes 8 servings

 1 package SIMPLY POTATOES® Homestyle Slices
 2 cans (15 ounces each) chili (no beans)
 1 package (16 ounces) jumbo hot dogs, cut into 1-inch pieces
 1 package (1 pound 3 ounces) refrigerated large flaky layer biscuits
 2 cups (8 ounces) CRYSTAL FARMS® Shredded Cheddar cheese

1. Heat oven to 350°F. Spray 13×9-inch glass baking dish with nonstick cooking spray. Spread potatoes in thin layer in bottom of baking dish. Top evenly with one can chili. Cover with aluminum foil; bake 30 minutes.

2. Uncover; top with hot dogs and remaining can chili. Separate biscuits; place over chili. Sprinkle with cheese. Continue baking, uncovered, 15 to 18 minutes or until biscuits are golden brown.

Rainbow Casserole

Harvest Helpings

Cheddar & Vegetable Pasta Bake

Makes 4 servings

- 2 tablespoons butter or margarine
- 2 cloves garlic, minced
- 1½ tablespoons all-purpose flour
- 1 can (12 ounces) evaporated skim milk
- ¾ teaspoon salt
- ½ teaspoon hot pepper sauce or ⅛ teaspoon cayenne pepper (optional)
- 2 cups (8 ounces) SARGENTO® Shredded Reduced Fat Mild Cheddar Cheese, divided
- 1 package (16 ounces) frozen mixed vegetables (cauliflower, red bell peppers, broccoli), thawed
- 3 cups (8 ounces) bow tie or penne pasta, cooked and drained

MELT butter in large saucepan over medium heat. Add garlic; cook 2 minutes. Add flour; cook and stir 1 minute. Add milk, salt and pepper sauce. Heat to a boil, stirring constantly. Remove from heat; stir in 1 cup cheese until melted.

ADD sauce and vegetables to pasta; toss well. Transfer to a greased medium baking dish or oval casserole. Cover with foil; bake in preheated 375°F oven 15 minutes or until hot. Uncover and sprinkle with remaining cheese; bake 2 minutes more or until cheese is melted.

Prep Time: 25 minutes • **Cook Time:** 17 minutes

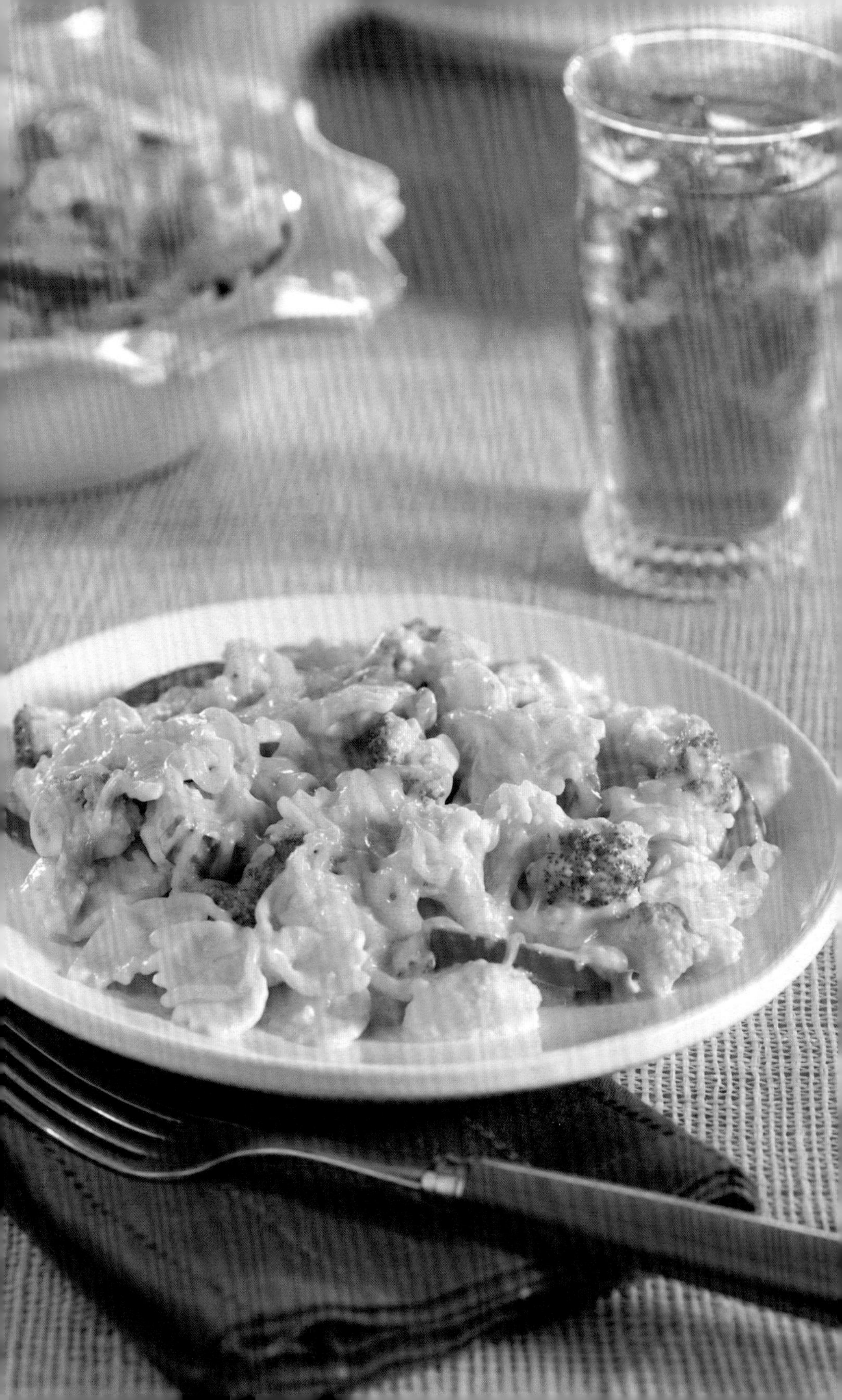

Beef & Zucchini Quiche

Makes 6 servings

 1 unbaked 9-inch pie crust
 8 ounces ground beef
 1 zucchini, shredded
 1 cup sliced mushrooms
 3 green onions, sliced
 1 tablespoon all-purpose flour
 1 cup milk
 3 eggs, beaten
 ¾ cup (3 ounces) shredded Swiss cheese
 1½ teaspoons chopped fresh thyme *or* ½ teaspoon dried thyme
 ½ teaspoon salt
   Dash black pepper
   Dash ground red pepper

1. Preheat oven to 475°F.

2. Line pie crust with foil; fill with dried beans or rice. Bake 8 minutes. Remove foil and beans. Bake 4 minutes; set aside. *Reduce oven temperature to 375°F.*

3. Brown beef in large skillet over medium-high heat 6 to 8 minutes, stirring to break up meat. Drain fat. Add zucchini, mushrooms and green onions; cook and stir until tender. Add flour; cook and stir 2 minutes. Remove from heat.

4. Combine milk, eggs, cheese, thyme, salt, black pepper and red pepper in medium bowl. Stir into beef mixture; pour into crust. Bake 35 minutes or until knife inserted into center comes out clean.

Beef & Zucchini Quiche

Salmon Casserole

Makes 8 servings

2 tablespoons butter
2 cups sliced mushrooms
1½ cups chopped carrots
1 cup frozen peas
1 cup chopped celery
½ cup chopped onion
½ cup chopped red bell pepper
1 tablespoon chopped fresh Italian parsley
1 clove garlic, minced
1 teaspoon salt
½ teaspoon black pepper
½ teaspoon dried basil
4 cups cooked rice
1 can (about 14 ounces) red salmon, drained and flaked
1 can (10¾ ounces) condensed cream of mushroom soup, undiluted
2 cups (8 ounces) shredded Cheddar cheese
½ cup sliced black olives

1. Preheat oven to 350°F. Lightly coat 2-quart casserole with nonstick cooking spray.

2. Melt butter in large saucepan or Dutch oven over medium heat. Add mushrooms, carrots, peas, celery, onion, bell pepper, parsley, garlic, salt, black pepper and basil; cook and stir 10 minutes or until vegetables are tender. Add rice, salmon, soup and cheese; mix well.

3. Transfer to prepared casserole; sprinkle with olives. Bake 30 minutes or until bubbly.

Salmon Casserole

Cauliflower Mac & Gouda

Makes 6 to 8 servings

1 package (about 16 ounces) bowtie pasta
4 cups milk
2 cloves garlic, peeled and smashed
¼ cup (½ stick) plus 3 tablespoons butter, divided
5 tablespoons all-purpose flour
1 pound Gouda cheese, shredded
1 teaspoon ground mustard
⅛ teaspoon smoked paprika or paprika
   Salt and black pepper
1 head cauliflower, cored and cut into florets
1 cup panko bread crumbs

1. Cook pasta according to package directions until almost tender. Drain pasta, reserving pasta water; keep warm. Return water to a boil.

2. Bring milk and garlic to a boil in small saucepan. Reduce heat; keep warm. Discard garlic.

3. Melt ¼ cup butter in large saucepan over medium heat; whisk in flour. Cook 1 minute, whisking constantly. Gradually add milk, whisking after each addition. Bring to a boil. Reduce heat; cook and stir 10 minutes or until thickened. Remove from heat.

4. Add cheese, mustard and paprika to sauce mixture; whisk until melted. Season with salt and pepper. Keep warm.

5. Preheat broiler. Add cauliflower to boiling pasta water. Cook 3 to 5 minutes or just until tender; drain. Toss pasta and cauliflower with sauce mixture. Spoon pasta mixture into 13×9-inch baking dish.

6. Melt remaining 3 tablespoons butter in small saucepan over medium heat. Add panko; stir just until moistened. Remove from heat. Sprinkle panko mixture over pasta mixture. Broil 2 minutes or until golden brown.

Cauliflower Mac & Gouda

Spinach-Potato Bake

Makes 6 servings

1 pound ground beef
1 onion, chopped
1 cup sliced mushrooms
2 cloves garlic, minced
1 package (10 ounces) frozen chopped spinach, thawed and
    squeezed dry
½ teaspoon ground nutmeg
1 pound russet potatoes, peeled, cooked and mashed
¼ cup sour cream
¼ cup milk
   Salt and black pepper
½ cup (2 ounces) shredded Cheddar cheese

1. Preheat oven to 400°F. Lightly coat 9-inch square baking dish with nonstick cooking spray.

2. Brown beef in large nonstick skillet over medium-high heat 6 to 8 minutes, stirring to break up meat. Drain all but 1 tablespoon fat. Add onion, mushrooms and garlic; cook and stir until tender. Stir in spinach and nutmeg. Cook until heated through, stirring occasionally.

3. Combine potatoes, sour cream and milk in medium bowl. Add to beef mixture; season with salt and pepper. Spoon into prepared baking dish; sprinkle with cheese.

4. Bake 15 to 20 minutes or until slightly puffed and cheese is melted.

Spinach-Potato Bake

Spicy Pork Chop Casserole

Makes 4 servings

Nonstick cooking spray
2 cups frozen corn
2 cups frozen diced hash brown potatoes
1 can (about 14 ounces) diced tomatoes with basil, garlic and
    oregano, drained
2 teaspoons chili powder
1 teaspoon dried oregano
½ teaspoon ground cumin
⅛ teaspoon red pepper flakes
1 teaspoon olive oil
4 boneless pork loin chops (about 3 ounces each), cut about
    ¾ inch thick
¼ teaspoon black pepper
¼ cup (1 ounce) shredded Monterey Jack cheese (optional)

1. Preheat oven to 375°F. Lightly coat 8-inch square baking dish with cooking spray.

2. Lightly spray large nonstick skillet with cooking spray. Add corn; cook and stir over medium-high heat 5 minutes or until corn begins to brown. Add potatoes; cook and stir 5 minutes or until potatoes begin to brown. Add tomatoes, chili powder, oregano, cumin and red pepper flakes; stir until blended. Transfer to prepared baking dish.

3. Heat oil in same skillet over medium-high heat. Add pork chops; cook until browned on one side. Place browned side up on top of corn mixture in baking dish. Sprinkle with black pepper.

4. Bake 20 minutes or until pork is barely pink in center. Sprinkle with cheese, if desired. Let stand 5 minutes before serving.

Prep Time: 15 minutes • **Bake Time:** 20 minutes

Spicy Pork Chop Casserole

Turkey Apple Cranberry Bake

Makes 4 servings

1 cup **PEPPERIDGE FARM®** Herb Seasoned Stuffing
1 tablespoon butter, melted
1 can (10¾ ounces) **CAMPBELL'S®** Condensed Cream of Celery Soup
   (Regular or 98% Fat Free)
½ cup milk
2 cups cubed cooked turkey
1 medium apple, diced (about 1½ cups)
1 stalk celery, finely chopped (about ½ cup)
½ cup dried cranberries
½ cup pecan halves, chopped

1. Stir the stuffing and butter in a small bowl. Set aside.

2. Stir the soup, milk, turkey, apple, celery, cranberries and pecans in a 12×8×2-inch shallow baking dish. Sprinkle the reserved stuffing mixture over the turkey mixture.

3. Bake at 400°F. for 30 minutes or until hot and bubbly.

Prep Time: 20 minutes • **Bake Time:** 30 minutes

Turkey Apple Cranberry Bake

Southwest Spaghetti Squash

Makes 4 servings

1 spaghetti squash (about 3 pounds)
1 can (about 14 ounces) Mexican-style diced tomatoes
1 can (about 14 ounces) black beans, rinsed and drained
¾ cup (3 ounces) shredded Monterey Jack cheese, divided
¼ cup finely chopped fresh cilantro
1 teaspoon ground cumin
¼ teaspoon garlic salt
¼ teaspoon black pepper

1. Preheat oven to 350°F. Spray baking sheet and 1½-quart baking dish with nonstick cooking spray. Cut squash in half lengthwise. Remove and discard seeds. Place squash, cut side down, on prepared baking sheet. Bake 45 minutes or just until tender. Shred hot squash with fork; place in large bowl. (Use oven mitts to protect hands.)

2. Add tomatoes, beans, ½ cup cheese, cilantro, cumin, garlic salt and pepper; toss well. Spoon mixture into prepared baking dish. Sprinkle with remaining ¼ cup cheese.

3. Bake 30 to 35 minutes or until heated through. Serve immediately.

TIP: This is a very simple, "kid-friendly" dish you can throw together in just a few minutes. It's great for those nights you want to go meatless!

Southwest Spaghetti Squash

Summer Squash Casserole

Makes 6 servings

2 cups sliced yellow squash
1 carrot, thinly sliced
½ cup chopped onion
½ cup diced red or green bell pepper
½ teaspoon salt
⅛ teaspoon black pepper
1 can (10¾ ounces) condensed cream of chicken or mushroom soup, undiluted
1 container (8 ounces) sour cream
1 cup (4 ounces) shredded Italian cheese blend
1 cup (4 ounces) shredded Cheddar cheese
1 package (6 ounces) stuffing mix

1. Preheat oven to 350°F. Combine squash, carrot, onion, bell pepper, salt and black pepper in medium saucepan; cover with water. Bring to a boil. Cook 5 minutes or until tender; drain.

2. Combine soup and sour cream in 13×9-inch baking dish; mix well. Stir in vegetable mixture. Sprinkle evenly with cheeses. Top with stuffing mix.

3. Cover; bake 30 minutes or until heated through.

Summer Squash Casserole

Turkey Meatball & Olive Casserole

Makes 6 servings

2 cups uncooked rotini pasta
8 ounces ground turkey
½ cup seasoned dry bread crumbs, divided
1 egg, lightly beaten
2 teaspoons dried minced onion
2 teaspoons Worcestershire sauce
½ teaspoon Italian seasoning
½ teaspoon salt
⅛ teaspoon black pepper
1 tablespoon vegetable oil
1 can (10¾ ounces) condensed cream of celery soup, undiluted
½ cup plain yogurt
¾ cup pimiento-stuffed green olives, sliced
1 tablespoon butter, melted
  Paprika (optional)

1. Preheat oven to 350°F. Spray 2-quart round casserole with nonstick cooking spray.

2. Cook pasta according to package directions until almost tender. Drain and set aside.

3. Meanwhile, combine turkey, ¼ cup bread crumbs, egg, onion, Worcestershire sauce, seasoning, salt and pepper in medium bowl. Shape mixture into ½-inch meatballs.

4. Heat oil in medium skillet over high heat. Add meatballs in single layer; cook until lightly browned on all sides.

5. Combine soup and yogurt in large bowl. Add pasta, meatballs and olives; stir gently to combine. Transfer to prepared casserole.

6. Combine remaining ¼ cup bread crumbs and butter in small bowl; sprinkle evenly over casserole. Sprinkle lightly with paprika, if desired.

7. Cover; bake 30 minutes. Uncover; bake 12 minutes or until meatballs are cooked through and casserole is bubbly.

Turkey Meatball & Olive Casserole

Sweet and Savory Sausage Casserole

Makes 4 to 6 servings

2 sweet potatoes, peeled and cut into 1-inch cubes
2 apples, peeled, cored and cut into 1-inch cubes
1 onion, cut into thin strips
2 tablespoons vegetable oil
2 teaspoons Italian seasoning
1 teaspoon garlic powder
½ teaspoon salt
½ teaspoon black pepper
1 pound Italian sausage, cooked and cut into ½-inch pieces

1. Preheat oven to 400°F. Lightly coat 13×9-inch baking dish with nonstick cooking spray.

2. Combine sweet potatoes, apples, onion, oil, seasoning, garlic powder, salt and pepper in large bowl; toss to coat evenly. Transfer to prepared baking dish.

3. Cover; bake 30 minutes. Add sausage; bake 10 minutes or until sausage is heated through and sweet potatoes are tender.

TIP: If you don't have Italian seasoning on your spice rack, you can substitute a blend of basil, oregano and parsley flakes.

Sweet and Savory Sausage Casserole

Farmhand Feasts

Beefy Texas Cheddar Bake

Makes 8 servings

1½ pounds ground beef
1 cup chopped onion
2 cans (10¾ ounces each) condensed tomato soup, preferably
   Mexican-style, undiluted
2 cups beef broth
1 package (6 ounces) corn bread stuffing mix
¼ cup (½ stick) butter, melted
2 teaspoons ground cumin
2 teaspoons chili powder
2 cups (8 ounces) shredded Mexican cheese blend

1. Preheat oven to 350°F. Lightly coat 3-quart casserole with nonstick cooking spray.

2. Brown beef in large nonstick skillet over medium-high heat 6 to 8 minutes, stirring to break up meat. Drain all but 1 tablespoon fat. Add onion; cook and stir 2 minutes or until translucent. Transfer to prepared casserole.

3. Mix soups, broth, stuffing mix, butter, cumin and chili powder in large bowl until combined. Spoon evenly over beef mixture. Top with cheese.

4. Bake 30 minutes or until heated through.

Ham, Poblano and Potato Casserole

Makes 6 servings

¼ cup (½ stick) butter
¼ cup all-purpose flour
1½ cups whole milk
2 pounds baking potatoes, halved and thinly sliced
6 ounces thinly sliced ham, cut into bite-size pieces
1 poblano pepper, cut into thin strips (about 1 cup)
1 cup corn
1 cup chopped red bell pepper
1 cup finely chopped onion
1½ teaspoons salt
¼ teaspoon black pepper
¼ teaspoon ground nutmeg
1½ cups (6 ounces) shredded sharp Cheddar cheese

1. Preheat oven to 350°F. Lightly coat 13×9-inch baking dish with nonstick cooking spray.

2. Melt butter in medium saucepan over medium heat. Add flour; whisk until smooth. Add milk; whisk until smooth. Cook and stir 5 to 7 minutes or until thickened. Remove from heat.

3. Layer one third of potatoes and half of ham, poblano pepper, corn, bell pepper and onion in prepared baking dish. Sprinkle with half of salt, black pepper and nutmeg. Repeat layers. Top with remaining one third of potatoes. Spoon white sauce evenly over all.

4. Cover with foil; bake 45 minutes. Uncover; bake 30 minutes or until potatoes are tender. Sprinkle with cheese; bake 5 minutes or until cheese is melted. Let stand 15 minutes before serving.

Note: To make this casserole even easier, use a food processor with the slicing blade attachment to thinly slice potatoes.

Ham, Poblano and Potato Casserole

Chile-Corn Quiche

Makes 6 servings

1 unbaked 9-inch pie crust
1 can (8¾ ounces) whole kernel corn, drained, *or* 1 cup frozen whole
    kernel corn, cooked
1 can (4 ounces) diced mild green chiles, drained
¼ cup thinly sliced green onions
1 cup (4 ounces) shredded Monterey Jack cheese
1½ cups half-and-half
3 eggs
½ teaspoon salt
½ teaspoon ground cumin

1. Preheat oven to 450°F.

2. Line crust with foil; fill with dried beans or rice. Bake 10 minutes. Remove foil and beans. Bake 5 minutes or until lightly browned. Let cool. *Reduce oven temperature to 375°F.*

3. Combine corn, chiles and green onions in small bowl. Spoon into crust; top with cheese. Whisk half-and-half, eggs, salt and cumin in medium bowl. Pour over cheese.

4. Bake 35 to 45 minutes or until filling is puffed and knife inserted into center comes out clean. Let stand 10 minutes before serving.

TIP: The mild heat of the green chiles combines with the sweetness of the corn and the richness of the Monterey Jack cheese to make this quiche incredibly delicious.

Chile-Corn Quiche

Creamy Beef, Carrot and Noodle Baked Stroganoff

Makes 6 servings

1 pound ground beef
1 large onion, diced (about 1 cup)
2 cans (10¾ ounces each) CAMPBELL'S® Condensed Cream of Mushroom Soup (Regular or 98% Fat Free)
2 cups water
2 cups frozen crinkle-cut carrots, thawed
2 cups uncooked medium egg noodles
½ cup sour cream

1. Cook the beef and onion in a 12-inch skillet until the beef is well browned, stirring frequently to separate meat. Pour off any fat. Spoon the beef mixture into a 13×9×2-inch (3-quart) shallow baking dish. Stir the soup, water, carrots, noodles and sour cream into the dish. **Cover.**

2. Bake at 375°F. for 30 minutes or until hot and bubbly.

Honey-Baked Heaven

Makes 6 servings

8 Granny Smith apples (or other tart apples), peeled and sliced
2 packages (8 ounces each) kielbasa sausage, cut into ½-inch slices
1⅓ cups honey
¼ cup water
1 tablespoon ground cinnamon
⅓ cup butter, cubed

1. Preheat oven to 350°F. Grease 13×9-inch baking dish.

2. Arrange apples and sausage in prepared baking dish.

3. Combine honey, water and cinnamon in medium bowl; mix well. Pour over apples and sausage. Dot with butter.

4. Bake 40 minutes or until apples are tender, basting with pan juices occasionally.

Creamy Beef, Carrot and Noodle Baked Stroganoff

Cha-Cha-Cha Casserole

Makes 6 servings

Nonstick cooking spray
1 can (about 7 ounces) whole green chiles, drained
1 pound ground turkey or chicken
1 cup chopped onion
3 cloves garlic, minced
1 tablespoon chili powder
1 teaspoon salt
1 teaspoon ground cumin
1 can (about 14 ounces) diced tomatoes with green chiles
2 cups thawed frozen corn
1 can (16 ounces) refried beans
2 cups (8 ounces) shredded Mexican cheese blend
2 cups crushed tortilla chips
1 cup chopped fresh tomato
½ cup sliced green onions

1. Preheat oven to 375°F. Spray 8-inch square baking dish with cooking spray. Cut chiles in half lengthwise; place in single layer in prepared baking dish.

2. Spray medium nonstick skillet with cooking spray; heat over medium heat. Add turkey, onion, garlic, chili powder, salt and cumin; cook and stir 5 minutes or until turkey is no longer pink. Stir in canned tomatoes; cook 10 minutes or until most of liquid evaporates.

3. Spoon turkey mixture over chiles; top with corn and beans. Sprinkle with cheese and crushed chips. Bake 30 minutes. Let stand 5 minutes. Sprinkle with fresh tomato and green onions just before serving.

Cha-Cha-Cha Casserole

Reuben Noodle Bake

Makes 6 servings

8 ounces uncooked egg noodles
5 ounces thinly sliced deli-style corned beef
1 can (about 14 ounces) sauerkraut with caraway seeds, drained
2 cups (8 ounces) shredded Swiss cheese
½ cup Thousand Island dressing
½ cup milk
1 tablespoon prepared mustard
2 slices pumpernickel bread
1 tablespoon butter, melted

1. Preheat oven to 350°F. Spray 13×9-inch baking dish with nonstick cooking spray.

2. Cook noodles according to package directions until almost tender. Drain.

3. Meanwhile, cut corned beef into bite-size pieces. Combine noodles, corned beef, sauerkraut and cheese in large bowl. Transfer to prepared baking dish.

4. Combine dressing, milk and mustard in small bowl. Spoon evenly over noodle mixture.

5. Tear bread into large pieces; process in food processor or blender until crumbs form. Combine bread crumbs and butter in small bowl; sprinkle evenly over casserole.

6. Bake 25 to 30 minutes or until heated through.

Vermont Harvest Mac-N-Cheese

Makes 5 servings

10 ounces elbow macaroni
3 tablespoons CABOT® Salted Butter
1 medium onion, finely chopped
1 to 2 cloves garlic, minced
1½ teaspoons minced fresh sage
3 tablespoons all-purpose flour
2 cups milk
3 cups grated CABOT® Extra Sharp Cheddar, divided
2½ cups diced smoked turkey
1½ cups diced apples
1½ cups croutons, lightly crushed

1. Preheat oven to 375°F. Butter 13×9-inch baking dish.

2. In large pot of boiling salted water, cook macaroni according to package directions; drain in colander and rinse briefly under cool water. Transfer elbows to prepared baking dish and set aside.

3. In large saucepan, melt butter. Add onion, garlic and sage; cook, stirring, until onion is tender. Stir in flour and cook over low heat for several minutes until very thick.

4. Gradually stir in milk. Cook, stirring, until sauce is simmering and slightly thickened. Add 2½ cups of cheese and stir just until melted.

5. Remove sauce from heat and stir in turkey and apples.

6. Pour over reserved elbows, stirring to combine. Top with crushed croutons and remaining ½ cup cheese. Bake for 25 to 30 minutes or until browned and bubbling.

Hearty Beef and Potato Casserole

Makes 6 servings

1 package (about 17 ounces) refrigerated fully cooked beef pot roast
    in gravy*
3 cups frozen hash brown potatoes
¼ teaspoon salt
¼ teaspoon black pepper
1 can (about 14 ounces) diced tomatoes
½ cup canned chipotle chile sauce
1 cup (4 ounces) shredded sharp Cheddar cheese

*Fully cooked beef pot roast in gravy can be found in the refrigerated prepared meats
section of the supermarket.

1. Preheat oven to 375°F. Lightly coat 11×7-inch baking dish with nonstick cooking spray.

2. Drain and discard gravy from pot roast. Cut beef into ¼-inch-thick slices. Place 2 cups potatoes in prepared baking dish. Sprinkle with salt and pepper. Top with beef. Combine tomatoes and chile sauce in small bowl; spread evenly over beef. Top with remaining 1 cup potatoes. Sprinkle with cheese.

3. Cover; bake 20 minutes. Uncover; bake 20 minutes or until bubbly. Let stand 5 minutes before serving.

Hearty Beef and Potato Casserole

Spicy Chicken Casserole with Corn Bread

Makes 4 to 6 servings

2 tablespoons olive oil
4 boneless skinless chicken breasts, cut into bite-size pieces
1 package (about 1 ounce) taco seasoning mix
1 can (about 15 ounces) black beans, rinsed and drained
1 can (about 14 ounces) diced tomatoes, drained
1 can (about 10 ounces) Mexican-style corn, drained
1 can (4 ounces) diced mild green chiles, drained
½ cup mild salsa
1 package (about 8 ounces) corn bread mix, plus ingredients to prepare mix
½ cup (2 ounces) shredded Cheddar cheese
¼ cup chopped red bell pepper

1. Preheat oven to 350°F. Lightly coat 2-quart casserole with nonstick cooking spray.

2. Heat oil in large skillet over medium heat. Cook and stir chicken until cooked through.

3. Sprinkle taco seasoning over chicken. Add beans, tomatoes, corn, chiles and salsa; stir until well blended. Transfer to prepared casserole.

4. Prepare corn bread mix according to package directions, adding cheese and bell pepper. Spread batter over chicken mixture.

5. Bake 30 minutes or until corn bread is golden brown.

Spicy Chicken Casserole with Corn Bread

Hearty Shepherd's Pie

Makes 6 servings

1½ pounds ground beef
2 cups *French's®* French Fried Onions
1 can (10¾ ounces) condensed tomato soup
½ cup water
2 teaspoons Italian seasoning
¼ teaspoon *each* salt and black pepper
1 package (10 ounces) frozen mixed vegetables, thawed
3 cups hot mashed potatoes

1. Preheat oven to 375°F.

2. Cook beef in large ovenproof skillet until browned; drain. Stir in *1 cup* French Fried Onions, soup, water, seasoning, salt and pepper.

3. Spoon vegetables over beef mixture. Top with mashed potatoes.

4. Bake 20 minutes or until hot. Sprinkle with remaining *1 cup* onions. Bake 2 minutes or until golden.

Prep Time: 10 minutes • **Cook Time:** 27 minutes

Hearty Shepherd's Pie

Tuna Tomato Casserole

Makes 6 servings

2 cans (6 ounces each) tuna, drained and flaked
1 cup mayonnaise
1 onion, finely chopped
¼ teaspoon salt
¼ teaspoon black pepper
1 package (12 ounces) wide egg noodles
8 to 10 plum tomatoes, sliced ¼ inch thick
1 cup (4 ounces) shredded Cheddar or mozzarella cheese

1. Preheat oven to 375°F.

2. Combine tuna, mayonnaise, onion, salt and pepper in medium bowl; mix well.

3. Cook noodles according to package directions. Drain and return to saucepan. Stir tuna mixture into noodles until well blended.

4. Layer half of noodle mixture, half of tomatoes and half of cheese in 13×9-inch baking dish. Press down slightly. Repeat layers.

5. Bake 20 minutes or until cheese is melted and casserole is heated through.

Pork-Stuffed Peppers

Makes 6 servings

1 pound ground pork
3 large green peppers
¼ cup raisins
½ cup chopped onion
½ cup chopped carrot
½ cup chopped celery
¼ teaspoon salt
1 cup cooked brown rice
2 tablespoons sunflower kernels
½ cup plain yogurt

Remove tops, seeds and membranes from peppers. Cut in half lengthwise. Cook in boiling salted water 5 minutes; drain.

Soak raisins in water 10 to 15 minutes; drain and set aside.

Combine pork, onion, carrot, celery and salt in medium skillet. Cook over low heat until pork is done and vegetables are tender, stirring occasionally. Drain thoroughly. Add rice, sunflower kernels, yogurt and raisins; mix well.

Spoon mixture into peppers. Place in 12×8×2-inch baking dish. Bake at 350°F 30 to 35 minutes or until heated through.

Prep Time: 20 minutes • **Cook Time:** 30 minutes

Favorite recipe from **National Pork Board**

Meat Crust Pie

Makes 8 servings

    1 pound ground beef
    2 cans (8 ounces each) tomato sauce, divided
    ½ cup seasoned dry bread crumbs
    ½ cup chopped green bell pepper, divided
    ¼ cup minced onion
    1 teaspoon salt, divided
    ⅛ teaspoon dried oregano
    ⅛ teaspoon black pepper
    1 cup water
 1⅓ cups uncooked instant rice
    1 cup (4 ounces) shredded Cheddar cheese, divided

1. Preheat oven to 350°F. Combine beef, ½ cup tomato sauce, bread crumbs, ¼ cup bell pepper, onion, ½ teaspoon salt, oregano and black pepper in large bowl; mix well. Pat onto bottom and up side of ungreased 9-inch deep-dish pie plate.

2. Bring water and remaining ½ teaspoon salt to a boil in medium saucepan. Stir in rice; cover and remove from heat. Let stand 5 minutes or until water is absorbed.

3. Add remaining 1½ cups tomato sauce, ½ cup cheese and remaining ¼ cup bell pepper to rice; mix well. Spoon rice mixture into meat crust. Cover with foil; bake 25 minutes.

4. Remove from oven and drain fat carefully, holding pan lid over top to keep pie from sliding. Top with remaining ½ cup cheese. Bake, uncovered, 10 to 15 minutes or until cheese is melted. Cut into wedges to serve.

Meat Crust Pie

Simple Suppers

One-Dish Chicken & Stuffing Bake

Makes 6 servings

4 cups PEPPERIDGE FARM® Herb Seasoned Stuffing
6 skinless, boneless chicken breast halves
  Paprika
1 can (10¾ ounces) CAMPBELL'S® Condensed Cream of Mushroom
    Soup (Regular or 98% Fat Free)
⅓ cup milk
1 tablespoon chopped fresh parsley or 1 teaspoon dried parsley flakes

1. Heat the oven to 400°F. Prepare the stuffing according to the package directions.

2. Spoon the stuffing across the center of a 3-quart shallow baking dish. Place the chicken on either side of the stuffing. Sprinkle the chicken with the paprika.

3. Stir the soup, milk and parsley in a small bowl. Pour the soup mixture over the chicken. Cover the baking dish.

4. Bake for 30 minutes or until the chicken is cooked through.

Kitchen Tip: 4 cups of any variety of PEPPERIDGE FARM® Stuffing will work in this recipe.

Prep Time: 15 minutes • **Bake Time:** 30 minutes

Potato Sausage Casserole

Makes 6 servings

1 pound bulk pork sausage or ground pork
1 can (10¾ ounces) condensed cream of mushroom soup, undiluted
¾ cup milk
½ cup chopped onion
½ teaspoon salt
¼ teaspoon black pepper
3 cups sliced potatoes
½ tablespoon butter, cut into small pieces
1½ cups (6 ounces) shredded Cheddar cheese
    Sliced green onions (optional)

1. Preheat oven to 350°F. Lightly coat 1½-quart casserole with nonstick cooking spray.

2. Brown sausage in large skillet over medium heat 6 to 8 minutes, stirring to break up meat. Drain fat.

3. Stir together soup, milk, onion, salt and pepper in medium bowl.

4. Place half of potatoes in prepared casserole. Top with half of soup mixture; top with half of sausage. Repeat layers, ending with sausage. Dot with butter.

5. Cover casserole with foil. Bake 1¼ to 1½ hours or until potatoes are tender. Uncover; sprinkle with cheese. Bake until cheese is melted and casserole is bubbly. Garnish with green onions.

Potato Sausage Casserole

Classic Turkey Pot Pie

Makes 8 servings

2 cans (15 ounces each) VEG•ALL® Original Mixed Vegetables, drained
1 can (10¾ ounces) condensed cream of potato soup, undiluted
¼ cup milk
1 pound cooked turkey, shredded (2 cups)
¼ teaspoon dried thyme
¼ teaspoon black pepper
2 (9-inch) refrigerated ready-to-bake pie crusts

Preheat oven to 375°F. In medium mixing bowl, combine first 6 ingredients; mix well. Place 1 pie crust into 9-inch pie pan; pour vegetable mixture into pie crust. Top with remaining crust, crimp edges to seal, and slit top with knife. Bake for 50 to 60 minutes (on lower rack) or until crust is golden brown and filling is hot. Allow pie to cool slightly before cutting into wedges to serve.

Speedy Mac & Cheese

Makes 6 servings

1 can (10¾ ounces) condensed Cheddar cheese soup
1 cup milk
4 cups hot cooked medium shell macaroni (3 cups uncooked)
1⅓ cups *French's®* French Fried Onions, divided
1 cup (4 ounces) shredded Cheddar cheese

MICROWAVE DIRECTIONS

Combine soup and milk in 2-quart microwavable casserole. Stir in macaroni, *⅔ cup* French Fried Onions and cheese. Cover; microwave on HIGH 10 minutes* or until heated through, stirring halfway through cooking time. Top with remaining *⅔ cup* onions. Microwave 1 minute or until onions are golden.

Or, bake, covered, in 350°F oven 25 to 30 minutes.

Prep Time: 10 minutes • **Cook Time:** 11 minutes

Classic Turkey Pot Pie

Smoky Mountain Chicken and Rice Casserole

Makes 8 to 10 servings

Vegetable cooking spray
2 cups sour cream
1 (10¾-ounce) can condensed cream of chicken soup
2 canned chipotle peppers in adobo sauce, finely chopped
1 teaspoon salt
1 teaspoon black pepper
3 cups cooked rice
2 cups shredded cooked chicken
2 cups shredded smoked Cheddar cheese

Preheat oven to 400°F. Lightly coat 13×9×2-inch baking dish with vegetable cooking spray. In large bowl, stir together sour cream, soup, chipotles, salt and black pepper until well blended. Stir in rice, chicken and cheese. Spoon into baking dish. Bake uncovered in preheated oven 20 to 25 minutes, until edges of casserole are bubbly. Turn oven to broil setting and lightly brown casserole.

Favorite recipe from **USA Rice**

TIP: If you have leftover chipotle peppers from the can you opened for this recipe, they can easily be frozen with the adobo sauce in a non-metal food storage container for later use.

Smoky Mountain Chicken and Rice Casserole

Zucchini, Chicken & Rice Casserole

Makes 4 servings

Vegetable cooking spray
1 package (12 ounces) refrigerated or thawed frozen breaded cooked
 chicken tenders, cut into bite-sized strips
2 large zucchini, cut in half lengthwise and thinly sliced (about
 4 cups)
1 jar (7 ounces) whole roasted sweet peppers, drained and thinly
 sliced
1 cup uncooked instant brown rice
1 can (10¾ ounces) CAMPBELL'S® Condensed Cream of Celery Soup
 (Regular or 98% Fat Free)
1 soup can water
½ cup sour cream

1. Heat the oven to 375°F. Spray a 3-quart shallow baking dish with
the cooking spray.

2. Stir the chicken, zucchini, peppers and rice in the baking dish.

3. Stir the soup, water and sour cream in a small bowl. Pour the soup
mixture over the chicken mixture. Cover the baking dish.

4. Bake for 35 minutes or until the rice is tender. Let stand for
10 minutes. Stir the rice before serving.

Prep Time: 15 minutes • **Bake Time:** 35 minutes

Zucchini, Chicken & Rice Casserole

Speedy Sirloin Steak Casserole

Makes 6 servings

1 (1½-pound) beef top sirloin steak, cut 1 inch thick
2 tablespoons extra virgin olive oil, divided
1 sheet refrigerated pie dough
1 teaspoon dried dill weed
½ teaspoon salt
1 medium onion, coarsely chopped
½ pound mushrooms, cut into quarters
1 tablespoon all-purpose flour
½ cup milk
1 teaspoon ground nutmeg
1 teaspoon beef bouillon granules
8 ounces (2 cups) shredded JARLSBERG® cheese
2 cups frozen peas

Cut beef into ¼-inch-thick slices. Cut each slice into 1-inch pieces. Combine with 1 tablespoon oil. Allow pie dough to stand at room temperature as package directs.

Heat large nonstick skillet until hot. Stir-fry beef mixture (half at a time) 1 to 2 minutes. Remove from skillet. Combine beef mixture, dill and salt; set aside.

Heat remaining 1 tablespoon oil in same skillet; add onion and cook until softened, about 3 to 4 minutes. Add mushrooms; cook 5 minutes, stirring frequently. Sprinkle with flour; cook 1 minute. Add milk, nutmeg and bouillon. Bring mixture to a boil and cook, stirring constantly, until mixture thickens. Add cheese; mix lightly until cheese melts. Stir in reserved beef mixture with accumulated juices and peas.

Spoon mixture into round 2-quart casserole. Fold pie crust edges under to fit inside edge of casserole; place on top of meat mixture. Crimp edges decoratively and cut slits in several places near center (to prevent cracking). Bake casserole in preheated 450°F oven 10 to 12 minutes or until crust is browned.

Prep Time: 30 minutes • **Cook Time:** 10 to 12 minutes

Carolina Baked Beans & Pork Chops

Makes 6 servings

 2 cans (16 ounces each) pork and beans
 ½ cup chopped onion
 ½ cup chopped green bell pepper
 ¼ cup *French's® Classic Yellow®* Mustard
 ¼ cup packed light brown sugar
 2 tablespoons *French's®* Worcestershire Sauce
 1 tablespoon *Frank's® RedHot®* Original Cayenne Pepper Sauce
 6 boneless pork chops (1 inch thick)

1. Preheat oven to 400°F. Combine all ingredients *except pork chops* in 3-quart shallow baking dish; mix well. Arrange chops on top, turning once to coat with sauce.

2. Bake, uncovered, 30 to 35 minutes or until pork is no longer pink in center. Stir beans around chops once during baking. Serve with green beans or mashed potatoes, if desired.

Prep Time: 10 minutes • **Cook Time:** 30 minutes

TIP: After purchasing pork chops, store them in the coldest part of the refrigerator no more than 2 to 3 days. If they are wrapped in butcher paper, they should be rewrapped in plastic wrap to prevent juices from leaking.

Country Chicken and Biscuits

Makes 4 servings

1 can (10¾ ounces) condensed cream of celery soup
⅓ cup milk or water
4 boneless, skinless chicken breast halves, cooked and cut into
    bite-sized pieces
1 can (14½ ounces) DEL MONTE® Cut Green Beans, drained
    Black pepper (optional)
1 can (11 ounces) refrigerated biscuits

1. Preheat oven to 375°F.

2. Combine soup and milk in large bowl. Gently stir in chicken and green beans; season with pepper, if desired. Spoon into 11×7-inch or 2-quart baking dish.

3. Cover with foil and bake at 375°F 20 to 25 minutes or until hot.

4. Separate biscuit dough into individual biscuits. Immediately arrange biscuits over hot mixture. Bake about 15 minutes or until biscuits are golden brown and baked through.

Microwave Directions: To prepare this dish even faster, use a microwavable baking dish in step 2. Cover with plastic wrap; slit to vent. Microwave on HIGH 8 to 10 minutes or until heated through, rotating dish once. Continue as directed in step 4.

Country Chicken and Biscuits

Wisconsin Swiss Ham and Noodles Casserole

Makes 6 to 8 servings

2 tablespoons butter
½ cup chopped onion
½ cup chopped green bell pepper
1 can (10½ ounces) condensed cream of mushroom soup
1 cup dairy sour cream
1 package (8 ounces) medium noodles, cooked and drained
2 cups (8 ounces) shredded Wisconsin Swiss cheese
2 cups cubed cooked ham (about ¾ pound)

In 1-quart saucepan, melt butter; sauté onion and bell pepper. Remove from heat; stir in soup and sour cream. In buttered 2-quart casserole, layer ⅓ of the noodles, ⅓ of the Swiss cheese, ⅓ of the ham and ½ soup mixture. Repeat layers, ending with final ⅓ layer of noodles, cheese and ham. Bake in preheated 350°F oven 30 to 45 minutes or until heated through.

Favorite recipe from **Wisconsin Milk Marketing Board**

Lamb & Stuffing Dinner Casserole

Makes 6 servings

2 tablespoons margarine
1 cup chopped onion
1 clove garlic, minced
1 can (14 ounces) reduced-sodium chicken broth, divided
1 cup coarsely shredded carrots
¼ cup fresh parsley, minced *or* 1 tablespoon dried parsley flakes
12 ounces cooked fresh American lamb, cut into cubes *or* 1 pound
   ground American lamb, cooked and drained
1 (6-ounce) box herb-flavored stuffing mix
1 (8-ounce) can whole tomatoes, drained and chopped

Melt margarine over medium heat; sauté onion and garlic 1 minute. Add ¼ cup broth, carrots and parsley. Cover and cook until carrots are crisp-tender, about 5 minutes. In large bowl, lightly combine lamb and stuffing mix. Add vegetable mixture, remaining broth and tomatoes. Toss lightly until well mixed.

Spoon lamb mixture into greased 8×8×2-inch baking dish. Cover and bake at 375°F for 20 minutes or until heated through.

Favorite recipe from **American Lamb Board**

Heartland Chicken Casserole

Makes 6 servings

    10 slices white bread, cubed
    1½ cups cracker crumbs or dry bread crumbs, divided
     4 cups cubed cooked chicken
     3 cups chicken broth
     1 cup chopped onion
     1 cup chopped celery
     1 can (8 ounces) sliced mushrooms, drained
     1 jar (about 4 ounces) pimientos, drained and diced
     3 eggs, lightly beaten
       Salt and black pepper
     1 tablespoon butter

1. Preheat oven to 350°F.

2. Combine bread cubes and 1 cup cracker crumbs in large bowl. Add chicken, broth, onion, celery, mushrooms, pimientos and eggs; mix well. Season with salt and pepper; spoon into 2½-quart casserole.

3. Melt butter in small saucepan over low heat. Add remaining ½ cup cracker crumbs; cook and stir until light brown. Sprinkle crumbs over casserole.

4. Bake 1 hour or until bubbly.

Heartland Chicken Casserole

Sausage, Beef & Bean Casserole

Makes 6 servings

1 pound sweet or hot Italian pork sausage, cut into 1-inch pieces
½ pound ground beef
1 small onion, chopped (about ¼ cup)
1 bag (6 ounces) fresh baby spinach leaves
1 can (10¾ ounces) CAMPBELL'S® Condensed Cream of Mushroom
    Soup (Regular or 98% Fat Free)
¼ cup milk
1 can (about 15 ounces) white kidney beans (cannellini), rinsed and
    drained
1 cup PEPPERIDGE FARM® Herb Seasoned Stuffing
½ cup crumbled blue cheese or shredded Cheddar cheese

1. Cook the sausage, beef and onion in a 12-inch nonstick skillet or 5-quart saucepot until the meats are well browned, stirring often to separate the meat. Pour off any fat. Add the spinach and cook until the spinach wilts.

2. Stir the soup, milk and beans into the skillet. Spoon the mixture into a 2-quart casserole.

3. Stir the stuffing and cheese in a small bowl. Sprinkle around the edge of the dish.

4. Bake at 350°F. for 30 minutes or until hot and bubbly and the internal temperature of the sausage mixture is 160°F.

Prep Time: 10 minutes • Bake Time: 30 minutes

Sausage, Beef & Bean Casserole

Monterey Chicken and Rice Quiche

Makes 6 servings

4 boneless, skinless chicken tenderloins, cut into 1-inch pieces
1¾ cups water
1 box UNCLE BEN'S® COUNTRY INN® Chicken & Vegetable Rice
1 cup frozen mixed vegetables
1 (9-inch) deep-dish ready-to-use frozen pie crust
3 eggs
½ cup milk
½ cup (2 ounces) shredded Monterey Jack cheese

1. Heat oven to 400°F.

2. In large skillet, combine chicken, water, rice, contents of seasoning packet and frozen vegetables. Bring to a boil. Cover; reduce heat and simmer 10 minutes. Spoon mixture into pie crust.

3. In small bowl, beat eggs and milk. Pour over rice mixture in pie crust; top with cheese. Bake 30 to 35 minutes or until knife inserted in center comes out clean.

Serving Suggestion: A fresh fruit compote of orange sections and green grapes or blueberries is the perfect accompaniment to this delicious quiche.

Monterey Chicken and Rice Quiche

Potluck Perfection

Kentucky Cornbread & Sausage Stuffing

Makes 6 to 8 servings

½ pound **BOB EVANS®** Original Recipe Roll Sausage
3 cups fresh bread cubes, dried or toasted
3 cups crumbled prepared cornbread
1 large apple, peeled and chopped
1 small onion, chopped
1 cup chicken or turkey broth
2 tablespoons minced fresh parsley
1 teaspoon salt
1 teaspoon rubbed sage or poultry seasoning
¼ teaspoon black pepper

Crumble sausage into small skillet. Cook over medium heat until browned, stirring occasionally. Place sausage and drippings in large bowl. Add remaining ingredients; toss lightly. Use to stuff chicken loosely just before roasting. Or, place stuffing in greased 13×9-inch baking dish. Add additional broth for moister stuffing, if desired. Bake in 350°F oven 30 minutes. Leftover stuffing should be removed from bird and stored separately in refrigerator. Reheat thoroughly before serving.

Company Crab

Makes 6 servings

    1 pound Florida blue crabmeat, fresh, frozen or pasteurized
    1 can (15 ounces) artichoke hearts, drained
    1 can (4 ounces) sliced mushrooms, drained
    2 tablespoons butter or margarine
2½ tablespoons all-purpose flour
  ½ teaspoon salt
  ⅛ teaspoon ground red pepper
    1 cup half-and-half
    2 tablespoons dry sherry
    2 tablespoons crushed cornflakes
    1 tablespoon grated Parmesan cheese
      Paprika

Preheat oven to 450°F. Thaw crabmeat if frozen. Remove any pieces of shell or cartilage. Cut artichoke hearts in half; place artichokes in well-greased shallow 1½-quart casserole. Add crabmeat and mushrooms; cover and set aside.

Melt butter in small saucepan over medium heat. Stir in flour, salt and ground red pepper. Gradually stir in half-and-half. Continue cooking until sauce thickens, stirring constantly. Stir in sherry. Pour sauce over crabmeat. Combine cornflakes and cheese in small bowl; sprinkle over casserole. Sprinkle with paprika. Bake 12 to 15 minutes or until bubbly.

Favorite recipe from **Florida Department of Agriculture and Consumer Services, Bureau of Seafood and Aquaculture**

Company Crab

Pasta & White Bean Casserole

Makes 6 servings

  1 tablespoon olive oil
  ½ cup chopped onion
  2 cloves garlic, minced
  2 cans (about 15 ounces each) cannellini beans, rinsed and drained
  3 cups cooked small shell pasta
  1 can (8 ounces) tomato sauce
1½ teaspoons Italian seasoning
  ½ teaspoon salt
  ½ teaspoon black pepper
  1 cup (4 ounces) shredded Italian cheese blend
  2 tablespoons finely chopped fresh Italian parsley

1. Preheat oven to 350°F. Lightly coat 2-quart casserole with nonstick cooking spray.

2. Heat oil in large skillet over medium-high heat. Add onion and garlic; cook and stir 4 minutes or until onion is tender.

3. Add beans, pasta, tomato sauce, seasoning, salt and pepper; mix well.

4. Transfer to prepared casserole; sprinkle with cheese and parsley. Bake 20 minutes or until cheese is melted.

Pasta & White Bean Casserole

Italian Sausage & Pasta Bake

Makes 6 servings

1 pound mild or hot Italian sausage
1 large onion, coarsely chopped
2 cloves garlic, minced
1 *each* large red and green bell peppers, cut into 1-inch squares
1 can (14½ ounces) diced tomatoes or Italian-style tomatoes,
   undrained
1 can (6 ounces) tomato paste
8 ounces ziti or mostaccioli pasta, cooked and drained
¼ cup chopped fresh basil or 2 teaspoons dried basil
2 cups (8 ounces) SARGENTO® Fancy Shredded 6 Cheese Italian
   Cheese, divided

CUT sausage into ½-inch pieces; discard casings. Cook sausage in large skillet over medium heat 5 minutes or until browned on all sides. Pour off drippings. Add onion, garlic and bell peppers; cook 5 minutes or until sausage is cooked through and vegetables are crisp-tender.

ADD tomatoes and tomato paste; mix well. Stir in pasta, basil and 1 cup cheese. Transfer to 13×9-inch baking dish. Cover and bake in preheated 375°F oven 20 minutes. Uncover; sprinkle remaining cheese evenly over casserole. Continue to bake 5 minutes or until cheese is melted.

Prep Time: 20 minutes • **Cook Time:** 25 minutes

Italian Sausage & Pasta Bake

Cheesy Tuna Pie

Makes 6 servings

  2 cups cooked rice
  2 cans (6 ounces each) tuna, drained and flaked
  1 cup mayonnaise
  1 cup (4 ounces) shredded Cheddar cheese
  ½ cup thinly sliced celery
  ½ cup sour cream
  1 can (4 ounces) sliced black olives
  2 tablespoons dried minced onion
  1 refrigerated pie crust dough

1. Preheat oven to 350°F. Spray 9-inch deep-dish pie pan with nonstick cooking spray.

2. Combine rice, tuna, mayonnaise, cheese, celery, sour cream, olives, and onion in medium bowl; mix well. Spoon into prepared pan. Top with pie dough; press edge to pan to seal. Cut slits for steam to escape.

3. Bake 20 minutes or until crust is browned and filling is bubbly.

TIP: This recipe is extremely adaptable. Try canned salmon instead of tuna or substitute an equal amount of your favorite cheese for the Cheddar. Once you master the basic recipe, you'll always be less than 30 minutes away from satisfying supper.

Cheesy Tuna Pie

Patchwork Casserole

Makes 8 to 10 servings

2 pounds ground beef
2 cups chopped green bell peppers
1 cup chopped onion
2 pounds frozen Southern-style hash brown potatoes, thawed
2 cans (8 ounces each) tomato sauce
1 cup water
1 can (6 ounces) tomato paste
1 teaspoon salt
½ teaspoon dried basil
¼ teaspoon black pepper
1 pound thinly sliced pasteurized process cheese product, divided

1. Preheat oven to 350°F.

2. Brown beef in large skillet over medium-high heat 6 to 8 minutes, stirring to break up meat. Drain all but 1 tablespoon fat. Add bell peppers and onion; cook and stir 4 minutes or until tender. Stir in potatoes, tomato sauce, water, tomato paste, salt, basil and black pepper.

3. Spoon half of mixture into 13×9-inch or 3-quart baking dish; top with half of cheese slices. Spoon remaining beef mixture evenly over top. Cover with foil; bake 45 minutes.

4. Cut remaining cheese slices into decorative shapes; place on top of casserole. Cover and let stand 5 minutes or until cheese is melted.

Country Scalloped Potatoes

Makes 6 servings

1 can (10¾ ounces) CAMPBELL'S® Condensed Cream of Celery Soup
    (Regular or 98% Fat Free)
1 can (10½ ounces) CAMPBELL'S® Chicken Gravy
1 cup milk
5 medium potatoes, peeled and thinly sliced (about 5 cups)
1 small onion, thinly sliced (about ¼ cup)
2½ cups diced cooked ham
1 cup shredded Cheddar cheese (about 4 ounces)

1. Stir the soup, gravy and milk in a small bowl. Layer **half** of the potatoes, onion, ham and soup mixture in a 3-quart shallow baking dish. Repeat the layers. Cover the baking dish.

2. Bake at 375°F. for 40 minutes. Uncover and bake for 25 minutes. Top with the cheese. Bake for 5 minutes or until the potatoes are tender and the cheese is melted. Let stand for 10 minutes.

Creamy Artichoke and Spinach Casserole

Makes 6 to 8 servings

½ cup finely chopped onion
½ cup (1 stick) butter
2 packages (10 ounces each) frozen chopped spinach, thawed and
    squeezed dry
1 can (14 ounces) artichoke hearts, drained and quartered
1½ cups plain yogurt
½ cup (2 ounces) grated Wisconsin Parmesan cheese
½ teaspoon salt
¼ teaspoon black pepper

In medium skillet, sauté onion in butter until tender; add remaining ingredients. Mix together; spread in 1½-quart casserole. Bake at 350°F 25 minutes.

Favorite recipe from **Wisconsin Milk Marketing Board**

Spicy Turkey Casserole

Makes 4 servings

    1 tablespoon olive oil
    1 pound turkey breast cutlets, cut into ½-inch pieces
    2 spicy turkey or chicken sausages (about 3 ounces each),
        cut into ½-inch-thick slices
    1 cup diced green bell pepper
    ½ cup sliced mushrooms
    ½ cup diced onion
    1 jalapeño pepper,* minced (optional)
    ½ cup chicken broth or water
    1 can (about 14 ounces) diced tomatoes
    1 cup cooked egg noodles
    1 teaspoon Italian seasoning
    ½ teaspoon paprika
    ¼ teaspoon black pepper
    6 tablespoons grated Parmesan cheese
    2 tablespoons coarse plain dry bread crumbs

*Jalapeño peppers can sting and irritate the skin, so wear rubber gloves when handling peppers and do not touch your eyes.

1. Preheat oven to 350°F. Heat oil in large nonstick skillet over medium heat. Add turkey and sausages; cook and stir 2 minutes.

2. Add bell pepper, mushrooms, onion and jalapeño pepper, if desired; cook and stir 5 minutes. Add broth; cook 1 minute, stirring to scrape up any browned bits. Add tomatoes, noodles, seasoning, paprika and black pepper; mix well.

3. Spoon turkey mixture into 10-inch shallow round casserole. Sprinkle with cheese and bread crumbs. Bake 15 to 20 minutes or until mixture is heated through and bread crumbs are golden brown.

Spicy Turkey Casserole

Broccoli-Rice Casserole

Makes 6 servings

Nonstick cooking spray
½ cup chopped onion
½ cup chopped celery
⅓ cup chopped red bell pepper
1 can (10¾ ounces) condensed broccoli and cheese soup, undiluted
¼ cup sour cream
2 cups cooked rice
1 package (10 ounces) frozen chopped broccoli, thawed and drained
1 tomato, cut into ¼-inch-thick slices

1. Preheat oven to 350°F. Lightly coat 1½-quart baking dish with cooking spray.

2. Coat large skillet with cooking spray; heat over medium heat. Add onion, celery and bell pepper; cook and stir until crisp-tender. Stir in soup and sour cream.

3. Layer rice and broccoli in prepared baking dish. Top with soup mixture, spreading evenly.

4. Cover with foil; bake 20 minutes. Top with tomato slices; bake, uncovered, 10 minutes.

Broccoli-Rice Casserole

Oniony Corn Spoonbread

Makes 8 servings

1 can (14¾ ounces) cream-style corn
1 can (11 ounces) Mexican-style corn
1 cup sour cream
1 package (6½ to 8½ ounces) corn muffin mix
½ cup diced red and green bell pepper
1 large egg
2 tablespoons butter or margarine, melted
1⅓ cups *French's*® French Fried Onions, divided
½ cup (2 ounces) shredded Cheddar cheese
Garnish: red bell pepper and chopped parsley (optional)

1. Preheat oven to 350°F. Combine corn, sour cream, corn muffin mix, bell peppers, egg, butter and ⅔ *cup* French Fried Onions. Pour mixture into greased shallow 2-quart baking dish.

2. Bake 40 minutes or until set. Top with cheese and remaining ⅔ *cup* onions; bake 5 minutes or until onions are golden. Garnish with bell pepper and parsley, if desired.

Variation: For added Cheddar flavor, substitute *French's*® Cheddar French Fried Onions for the original flavor.

Prep Time: 5 minutes • **Cook Time:** 45 minutes

Oniony Corn Spoonbread

Hot Three-Bean Casserole

Makes 12 servings

    2 tablespoons olive oil
    1 cup coarsely chopped onion
    1 cup chopped celery
    2 cloves garlic, minced
    1 can (about 15 ounces) chickpeas, rinsed and drained
    1 can (about 15 ounces) kidney beans, rinsed and drained
    1 cup coarsely chopped tomato
    1 can (8 ounces) tomato sauce
    1 cup water
    1 to 2 jalapeño peppers,* minced
    1 tablespoon chili powder
    2 teaspoons sugar
 1½ teaspoons ground cumin
    1 teaspoon salt
    1 teaspoon dried oregano
    ¼ teaspoon black pepper
 2½ cups (10 ounces) frozen cut green beans
       Fresh oregano (optional)

Jalapeño peppers can sting and irritate the skin, so wear rubber gloves when handling peppers and do not touch your eyes.

1. Heat oil in large skillet over medium heat. Add onion, celery and garlic; cook and stir 5 minutes or until tender.

2. Add chickpeas, beans, tomato, tomato sauce, water, jalapeño pepper, chili powder, sugar, cumin, salt, dried oregano and black pepper. Bring to a boil. Reduce heat to low; simmer 20 minutes.

3. Add green beans; simmer 10 minutes or until tender. Garnish with fresh oregano.

Hot Three-Bean Casserole

Country Sausage Macaroni and Cheese

Makes 6 to 8 servings

  1 pound BOB EVANS® Special Seasonings Roll Sausage
1½ cups milk
 12 ounces pasteurized processed Cheddar cheese, cut into cubes
 ½ cup Dijon mustard
  1 cup diced fresh or drained canned tomatoes
  1 cup sliced mushrooms
 ⅓ cup sliced green onions
 ⅛ teaspoon cayenne pepper
 12 ounces uncooked elbow macaroni
  2 tablespoons grated Parmesan cheese

Preheat oven to 350°F. Crumble and cook sausage in medium skillet until browned. Drain on paper towels. Combine milk, processed cheese and mustard in medium saucepan; cook and stir over low heat until cheese melts and mixture is smooth. Stir in sausage, tomatoes, mushrooms, green onions and cayenne pepper. Remove from heat.

Cook macaroni according to package directions; drain. Combine hot macaroni and cheese mixture in large bowl; toss until well coated. Spoon into greased shallow 2-quart casserole dish. Cover and bake 15 to 20 minutes. Stir; sprinkle with Parmesan cheese. Bake, uncovered, 5 minutes more. Let stand 10 minutes before serving. Refrigerate leftovers.

Country Sausage Macaroni and Cheese

Meatball Stroganoff

Makes 4 servings

1 can (10¾ ounces) condensed cream of mushroom soup, undiluted
1 container (8 ounces) sour cream
1 cup milk
1 package (15 ounces) frozen prepared meatballs, thawed and cut
    in half if large
4 cups cooked egg noodles (5 ounces uncooked)
1 cup (4 ounces) shredded Swiss cheese
2 cups *French's®* French Fried Onions, divided
¼ cup minced fresh parsley
1 tablespoon *French's®* Worcestershire Sauce
1 teaspoon paprika

1. Preheat oven to 350°F. Coat 3-quart shallow baking dish with vegetable cooking spray.

2. Combine soup, sour cream and milk in large bowl. Stir in meatballs, noodles, cheese, *1 cup* French Fried Onions, parsley, Worcestershire and paprika. Spoon into prepared baking dish.

3. Bake 25 minutes or until heated through. Stir. Sprinkle with remaining *1 cup* onions; bake 5 minutes or until onions are golden brown.

Prep Time: 10 minutes • **Cook Time:** 30 minutes

Acknowledgments

The publisher would like to thank the companies and organizations listed below for the use of their recipes and photographs in this publication.

American Lamb Board

Bob Evans®

Cabot® Creamery Cooperative

Campbell Soup Company

Cream of Wheat® Cereal

Del Monte Foods

Florida Department of Agriculture and Consumer Services, Bureau of Seafood and Aquaculture

Kraft Foods Global, Inc.

MASTERFOODS USA

Michael Foods, Inc.

National Pork Board

Norseland, Inc.

Reckitt Benckiser Inc.

Sargento® Foods Inc.

USA Rice Federation®

Veg•All®

Wisconsin Milk Marketing Board

A

Apple
Apple-Cranberry Kugel, 6
Cheddar Apple Breakfast Lasagna, 10
Honey-Baked Heaven, 78
Kentucky Cornbread & Sausage Stuffing, 116
Sweet and Savory Sausage Casserole, 70
Turkey Apple Cranberry Bake, 62
Vermont Harvest Mac-N-Cheese, 83

B

Bacon
Bacon and Eggs Brunch Casserole, 20
Spinach Sensation, 12
Beans
Carolina Baked Beans & Pork Chops, 105
Cha-Cha-Cha Casserole, 80
Country Chicken and Biscuits, 106
Family-Style Frankfurters with Rice and Red Beans, 32
Hot Three-Bean Casserole, 134
Pasta & White Bean Casserole, 120
Sausage, Beef & Bean Casserole, 112
Southwest Spaghetti Squash, 64
Spicy Chicken Casserole with Corn Bread, 86
Beef (*see also* **Beef, Ground**)
Hearty Beef and Potato Casserole, 84
Reuben Noodle Bake, 82
Speedy Sirloin Steak Casserole, 104
Beef, Ground
Beef & Zucchini Quiche, 52
Beefy Texas Cheddar Bake, 72
Creamy Beef, Carrot and Noodle Baked Stroganoff, 78
Hearty Shepherd's Pie, 88
Meatball Stroganoff, 138
Meat Crust Pie, 92

Beef, Ground (*continued*)
Patchwork Casserole, 126
Pizza Roll-Ups, 30
Rainbow Casserole, 48
Sausage, Beef & Bean Casserole, 112
Spinach-Potato Bake, 58
Stroganoff Casserole, 44
Beef & Zucchini Quiche, 52
Beefy Texas Cheddar Bake, 72
Blueberry-Orange French Toast Casserole, 14
Breakfast Bake, 16
Broccoli
Broccoli-Rice Casserole, 130
Crustless Salmon & Broccoli Quiche, 4
Homestyle Chicken & Rice Casserole, 38

C

Carolina Baked Beans & Pork Chops, 105
Cauliflower Mac & Gouda, 56
Cha-Cha-Cha Casserole, 80
Cheddar & Vegetable Pasta Bake, 50
Cheddar Apple Breakfast Lasagna, 10
Cheesy Tuna Pie, 124
Chicken
Chicken Pot Pie with Onion Biscuits, 26
Country Chicken and Biscuits, 106
Heartland Chicken Casserole, 110
Homestyle Chicken & Rice Casserole, 38
Monterey Chicken and Rice Quiche, 114
One-Dish Chicken & Stuffing Bake, 94
Smoky Mountain Chicken and Rice Casserole, 100
Spicy Chicken Casserole with Corn Bread, 86
Zucchini, Chicken & Rice Casserole, 102

Chile-Corn Quiche, 76
Chili Dog Casserole, 48
Chili Wagon Wheel Casserole, 40
City Pork BBQ Casserole, 36
Classic Turkey Pot Pie, 98
Company Crab, 118
Corn
  Cha-Cha-Cha Casserole, 80
  Chile-Corn Quiche, 76
  Fruited Corn Pudding, 22
  Ham, Poblano and Potato Casserole,
    74
  Oniony Corn Spoonbread, 132
  Spicy Chicken Casserole with Corn
    Bread, 86
  Spicy Pork Chop Casserole, 60
Country Chicken and Biscuits, 106
Country Sausage Macaroni and
    Cheese, 136
Country Scalloped Potatoes, 127
Cranberry
  Apple-Cranberry Kugel, 6
  Turkey Apple Cranberry Bake, 62
Creamy Artichoke and Spinach
    Casserole, 127
Creamy Beef, Carrot and Noodle Baked
    Stroganoff, 78
Crustless Salmon & Broccoli Quiche, 4

E
Egg and Green Chile Rice Casserole,
    18
Egg & Sausage Casserole, 24

F
Family-Style Frankfurters with Rice
    and Red Beans, 32
Fish and Shellfish
  Cheesy Tuna Pie, 124
  Company Crab, 118
  Crustless Salmon & Broccoli Quiche,
    4
  Louisiana Seafood Bake, 46
  Salmon Casserole, 54
  Tuna Tomato Casserole, 90
  Velveeta® Tuna Noodle Casserole,
    34
Fruited Corn Pudding, 22

H
Ham
  Cheddar Apple Breakfast Lasagna,
    10
  Country Scalloped Potatoes, 127
  Ham & Cheese Grits Soufflé, 20
  Ham, Poblano and Potato Casserole,
    74
  Wisconsin Swiss Ham and Noodles
    Casserole, 108
Heartland Chicken Casserole, 110
Hearty Beef and Potato Casserole,
    84
Hearty Sausage & Rice Casserole,
    42
Hearty Shepherd's Pie, 88
Homestyle Chicken & Rice Casserole,
    38
Honey-Baked Heaven, 78
Hot Three-Bean Casserole, 134

I
Italian Sausage & Pasta Bake, 122

K
Kentucky Cornbread & Sausage
    Stuffing, 116

L
Lamb & Stuffing Dinner Casserole,
    109
Louisiana Seafood Bake, 46

M
Meatball Stroganoff, 138
Meat Crust Pie, 92
Monterey Chicken and Rice Quiche,
    114
Mushrooms
  Beef & Zucchini Quiche, 52
  Company Crab, 118
  Country Sausage Macaroni and
    Cheese, 136
  Heartland Chicken Casserole, 110
  Hearty Sausage & Rice Casserole,
    42
  Salmon Casserole, 54
  Speedy Sirloin Steak Casserole, 104

Mushrooms *(continued)*
Spicy Turkey Casserole, 128
Spinach-Potato Bake, 58
Stroganoff Casserole, 44

O
One-Dish Chicken & Stuffing Bake, 94
Oniony Corn Spoonbread, 132

P
Pasta and Noodles
Apple-Cranberry Kugel, 6
Cauliflower Mac & Gouda, 56
Cheddar & Vegetable Pasta Bake, 50
Chili Wagon Wheel Casserole, 40
Country Sausage Macaroni and Cheese, 136
Creamy Beef, Carrot and Noodle Baked Stroganoff, 78
Italian Sausage & Pasta Bake, 122
Meatball Stroganoff, 138
Pasta & White Bean Casserole, 120
Pizza Roll-Ups, 30
Reuben Noodle Bake, 82
Speedy Mac & Cheese, 98
Spicy Turkey Casserole, 128
Stroganoff Casserole, 44
Tuna Tomato Casserole, 90
Turkey Meatball & Olive Casserole, 68
Velveeta® Tuna Noodle Casserole, 34
Vermont Harvest Mac-N-Cheese, 83
Wisconsin Swiss Ham and Noodles Casserole, 108
Pasta & White Bean Casserole, 120
Patchwork Casserole, 126
Pizza Roll-Ups, 30
Pork *(see also* **Bacon; Ham; Sausage***)*
Carolina Baked Beans & Pork Chops, 105
City Pork BBQ Casserole, 36
Pork and Corn Bread Stuffing Casserole, 28

Pork *(continued)*
Pork-Stuffed Peppers, 91
Spicy Pork Chop Casserole, 60
Potatoes
Chili Dog Casserole, 48
Country Scalloped Potatoes, 127
Egg & Sausage Casserole, 24
Ham, Poblano and Potato Casserole, 74
Hearty Beef and Potato Casserole, 84
Hearty Shepherd's Pie, 88
Patchwork Casserole, 126
Potato Sausage Casserole, 96
Rainbow Casserole, 48
Spicy Pork Chop Casserole, 60
Spinach-Potato Bake, 58
Sweet and Savory Sausage Casserole, 70
Potato Sausage Casserole, 96

R
Rainbow Casserole, 48
Reuben Noodle Bake, 82
Rice
Broccoli-Rice Casserole, 130
Cheesy Tuna Pie, 124
City Pork BBQ Casserole, 36
Egg and Green Chile Rice Casserole, 18
Family-Style Frankfurters with Rice and Red Beans, 32
Hearty Sausage & Rice Casserole, 42
Homestyle Chicken & Rice Casserole, 38
Louisiana Seafood Bake, 46
Meat Crust Pie, 92
Monterey Chicken and Rice Quiche, 114
Pork-Stuffed Peppers, 91
Salmon Casserole, 54
Smoky Mountain Chicken and Rice Casserole, 100
Zucchini, Chicken & Rice Casserole, 102
Roasted Pepper and Sourdough Brunch Casserole, 8

S
Salmon Casserole, 54
Sausage
  Breakfast Bake, 16
  Chili Dog Casserole, 48
  Country Sausage Macaroni and
    Cheese, 136
  Egg & Sausage Casserole, 24
  Family-Style Frankfurters with Rice
    and Red Beans, 32
  Hearty Sausage & Rice Casserole,
    42
  Honey-Baked Heaven, 78
  Italian Sausage & Pasta Bake,
    122
  Kentucky Cornbread & Sausage
    Stuffing, 116
  Potato Sausage Casserole, 96
  Sausage, Beef & Bean Casserole,
    112
  Spicy Turkey Casserole, 128
  Sweet and Savory Sausage
    Casserole, 70
Smoky Mountain Chicken and Rice
    Casserole, 100
Southwest Spaghetti Squash, 64
Speedy Mac & Cheese, 98
Speedy Sirloin Steak Casserole, 104
Spicy Chicken Casserole with Corn
    Bread, 86
Spicy Pork Chop Casserole, 60
Spicy Turkey Casserole, 128
Spinach
  Creamy Artichoke and Spinach
    Casserole, 127
  Sausage, Beef & Bean Casserole,
    112
  Spinach-Potato Bake, 58
  Spinach Sensation, 12
Stroganoff Casserole, 44
Stuffing Mix
  Beefy Texas Cheddar Bake, 72
  Lamb & Stuffing Dinner Casserole,
    109
  One-Dish Chicken & Stuffing Bake,
    94
  Pork and Corn Bread Stuffing
    Casserole, 28

Stuffing Mix (continued)
  Sausage, Beef & Bean Casserole,
    112
  Summer Squash Casserole, 66
  Turkey Apple Cranberry Bake, 62
Summer Squash Casserole, 66
Sweet and Savory Sausage Casserole,
    70

T
Tuna Tomato Casserole, 90
Turkey
  Cha-Cha-Cha Casserole, 80
  Chili Wagon Wheel Casserole, 40
  Classic Turkey Pot Pie, 98
  Spicy Turkey Casserole, 128
  Turkey Apple Cranberry Bake, 62
  Turkey Meatball & Olive Casserole,
    68
  Vermont Harvest Mac-N-Cheese,
    83

V
Velveeta® Tuna Noodle Casserole,
    34
Vermont Harvest Mac-N-Cheese,
    83

W
Wisconsin Swiss Ham and Noodles
    Casserole, 108

Z
Zucchini
  Beef & Zucchini Quiche, 52
  Zucchini, Chicken & Rice Casserole,
    102

METRIC CONVERSION CHART

VOLUME MEASUREMENTS (dry)

1/8 teaspoon = 0.5 mL
1/4 teaspoon = 1 mL
1/2 teaspoon = 2 mL
3/4 teaspoon = 4 mL
1 teaspoon = 5 mL
1 tablespoon = 15 mL
2 tablespoons = 30 mL
1/4 cup = 60 mL
1/3 cup = 75 mL
1/2 cup = 125 mL
2/3 cup = 150 mL
3/4 cup = 175 mL
1 cup = 250 mL
2 cups = 1 pint = 500 mL
3 cups = 750 mL
4 cups = 1 quart = 1 L

VOLUME MEASUREMENTS (fluid)

1 fluid ounce (2 tablespoons) = 30 mL
4 fluid ounces (1/2 cup) = 125 mL
8 fluid ounces (1 cup) = 250 mL
12 fluid ounces (1 1/2 cups) = 375 mL
16 fluid ounces (2 cups) = 500 mL

WEIGHTS (mass)

1/2 ounce = 15 g
1 ounce = 30 g
3 ounces = 90 g
4 ounces = 120 g
8 ounces = 225 g
10 ounces = 285 g
12 ounces = 360 g
16 ounces = 1 pound = 450 g

DIMENSIONS

1/16 inch = 2 mm
1/8 inch = 3 mm
1/4 inch = 6 mm
1/2 inch = 1.5 cm
3/4 inch = 2 cm
1 inch = 2.5 cm

OVEN TEMPERATURES

250°F = 120°C
275°F = 140°C
300°F = 150°C
325°F = 160°C
350°F = 180°C
375°F = 190°C
400°F = 200°C
425°F = 220°C
450°F = 230°C

BAKING PAN SIZES

Utensil	Size in Inches/Quarts	Metric Volume	Size in Centimeters
Baking or	8×8×2	2 L	20×20×5
Cake Pan	9×9×2	2.5 L	23×23×5
(square or	12×8×2	3 L	30×20×5
rectangular)	13×9×2	3.5 L	33×23×5
Loaf Pan	8×4×3	1.5 L	20×10×7
	9×5×3	2 L	23×13×7
Round Layer	8×1½	1.2 L	20×4
Cake Pan	9×1½	1.5 L	23×4
Pie Plate	8×1¼	750 mL	20×3
	9×1¼	1 L	23×3
Baking Dish	1 quart	1 L	—
or Casserole	1½ quart	1.5 L	—
	2 quart	2 L	—